Daily Telegraph

EDUCATION
A-Z

JOHN IZBICKI

Collins
London and Glasgow

William Collins Sons & Co. Ltd.
London & Glasgow

First published 1978

© *The Daily Telegraph*
ISBN 0 00 412070 1 (limp)
ISBN 0 00 412069 8 (cased)

Printed in Great Britain

Introduction

Prime Ministers rarely, if ever, speak on education. Few of them, if any, know very much about the subject. It was, therefore, quite unprecedented for James Callaghan to devote his entire speech at Ruskin College, Oxford, on 18 October 1976, to educational standards and what the country ought to be doing about them. He was really doing no more than echoing the opinions of many thousands of parents, teachers and educationists who, over the past ten years or so have become increasingly concerned over the state of our schools and colleges and what was happening to the children of this country.

James Callaghan's initiative became the curtain raiser to what was to become known as the 'Great Debate'. Throughout most of 1977, regional conferences organized by the Department of Education and Science and, quite separately, by the Conservative party's parliamentary education committee, were held in numerous parts of the country. Chaired by Shirley Williams, Secretary of State for Education, or her two deputies, Gordon Oakes, Minister of State, and Margaret Jackson, Under-Secretary of State (the Tory-organized debates were chaired by Norman St John-Stevas, chief Opposition spokesman on education, and his number two, Dr Rhodes Boyson) these conferences gave people an opportunity to speak frankly about a multitude of problems: the curriculum, standards of reading, writing and arithmetic, the standard of teacher training and in-service courses, the relationship between education and industry, how children were taught (if at all) to cope with the outside world, with work, with life – and so on.

People were becoming worried (and, so far, nothing much has happened to dispel their fears) about declining standards and the fact that employers were not satisfied with the kind of material being churned out by the schools. School leavers were found not only to have little knowledge about the world of work but were often unable even to write a reasonable letter of application for a job. Spelling was atrocious, grammar almost non-existent and punctuation a disgrace. What, employers – not unreasonably – wanted to know, had these children been taught at their schools?

As for teachers, were they any better? Parents complained that their children's reports from school had been badly written and teachers' comments contained some of the most awful howlers: 'Johnny shud try harder'; 'Helen is comming on niecly'; 'His dissiplin leaves much to be desired'; 'Her homework is offen very untiedy' and so on.

Was it any wonder, parents and employers commented, that the country was in its present mess? Certainly, Britain had no time for complacency. She could boast of very little raw material – a sprinkling of coal, a trickle of oil – except one: brains. Brains were the only assets being produced by this once great island; unless parents, teachers, and the teachers of teachers were prepared to nurture those brains, the country might just as well pull down its shutters altogether.

This then was the basis for the Great Debate: to examine what was wrong with our education system, to see how it had gone wrong and to propose ways and means of improving it and eventually solving the problem.

Are things really as bad as all that? After all, more and more youngsters are passing examinations and gaining degrees. In just one decade (1965–75) the percentage of school leavers who had managed to gain two or more Advanced level passes in the General Certificate of Education had risen from ten per cent to twelve per cent. The number of people starting degree courses at universities and polytechnics had jumped from 36,000 in 1965 to 46,000 in 1975. The number of girls embarking on degree courses had almost doubled over the same period – from 10,000 in 1965 to more than 17,000 in 1975.

So much for the good news. The number leaving school qualified to enter higher or further education with two or more A-levels represents about one-fifth of the 718,000 school leavers in 1975. A further sixty per cent left with some kind of qualification in their pockets – either a GCE Ordinary level (or possibly more than one such O-level) or one or more successes in the CSE – Certificate of Secondary Education.

But about 144,000 children (roughly twenty per cent) of the school leavers in 1975 had sat no public examination at all, whether GCE or CSE. They held no qualifications and, things being as they are, they mostly went straight on to the dole, the failures of contemporary society.

It would be wrong to assume that this last category represented a decline in standards (whatever that might mean on its own), for the percentage of unqualified leavers has dropped almost phenomenally over the past decade. Until 1965, about eighty per cent of pupils aged sixteen were excluded from public examinations. Today, about eighty per cent sit them.[1]

Yet, however unfair it might be to label 144,000 school leavers as 'failures' simply because they cannot wave a piece of paper before the noses of prospective employers, the fact remains that these children augment the queues of unemployed since few employers even wish to interview anyone without such a piece of paper.

And what of that piece of paper – that sixty per cent category who leaves school with one or more CSEs or GCE O-levels? What value can be attached to four CSEs at Grade 5 or two O-levels at Grade D? Indeed, how many employers bother at all with applicants who state that they have a whole batch of CSEs, even at reasonably good grades. How many know or care that a CSE Grade 1 is equivalent to an O-level pass? What they are likely to care about very much indeed is whether the letter of application for the job in question has been well or badly written, whether it is neat, whether it has many crossings out that have almost gone through the paper and whether there are fewer or more than half a dozen spelling mistakes. Many will care (and rightly so) whether a letter which starts off 'Dear Sir' is signed 'Yours sincerely' or 'Yours faithfully.'

And many employers will also take note of whether candidates for jobs are able to add and subtract, divide and multiply reasonably easy numbers. Many witnesses giving evidence to the Parliamentary Select Committee on the Attainments of the School Leaver complained about the 'absence of even the most rudimentary arithmetical skills in some of their recruits', and the Department of Employment cited figures that would make the hair of many an employer (or parent) stand on end. The Department gave a 20-item test in multiple-choice form to test the ability of 1549 children to handle the four basic arithmetical rules. 'Many of the items should be comfortably within the grasp of primary school children,' the evidence stated. Of course, the difference was that these were not primary school children but sixteen-year-old school leavers.

Nearly fifteen per cent (about 230 of the 1549 children) 'failed to get several quite simple sums right, involving the addition of three-figure numbers or the division of a single number into a three-figure number where there is no remainder.

1 Evidence given by Mr R. Christopher of the Joint Matriculation Board to the Education, Arts and Home Office Sub-Committee of the Parliamentary Expenditure Committee (Para. 27 in the Committee's Tenth Report, published 14 September, 1977 as House of Commons Paper 525).

'Although the multiple choice form whereby five possible answers are given and the candidate merely circles the correct one, allows even a guesser to obtain about four out of twenty by chance alone, eleven per cent of children tested scored five or less.

'It is difficult to avoid the conclusion, that so far as basic arithmetical skills are concerned, something like one in nine of the school leavers tested cannot be said to have the competence of the average junior school leaver.'[2]

This conclusion was not reached by any Black Paper writer but by a group of MPs representing all political parties. It is a conclusion that must be taken seriously by all those concerned with the education of our children.

The Three Rs are not alone in decline [and children cannot be blamed entirely for their inability to spell when confronted daily with the idiotic spelling of advertising copywriters (Beanz Meanz Heinz and similar atrocities of language) nor can teachers take the entire responsibility when that other white elephant of education, the Schools Council, has decided that grammar should no longer be examinable] though one should question why so many children are being transferred from primary to secondary schools still unable to read and write fluently.

At Sixth Form level there is another growing problem to face. Should pupils be taught subjects that will be useful to the country's needs or should we allow sixth formers to choose those subjects they actually like? There was a time when the country needed chemists desperately. Within a few short years, Britain had a glut of chemists and new graduates were having to turn their talents to other jobs. We once, not long ago, needed teachers. Out went the cry for married women to return to teaching; five O-levels sufficed for the college of education applicant to gain a place; hardly anyone failed their qualifying examinations. By 1977 there were 20,000 teachers on the dole. The reason for the sudden over-production of teachers was a miscalculation on the part of statisticians. They had not reckoned on a fall in the birth rate, thanks mainly to the Pill, and had projected figures too far ahead.

Mr Callaghan in his Ruskin speech referred to the need for more engineers. No doubt there will be unemployment among engineers within the next five years.

The mistake made all too often is that politicians and statisticians talk in terms of *numbers*. 'We need *more* this, that or the other' and

2 *Ibid*, Para 34.

not 'We need *better* . . .' Take, for example the Callaghan plea for more engineers, or the previous call for more teachers. I am convinced that numerically there are quite enough engineers and teachers about. I am equally convinced that there are insufficient *good* engineers or teachers.

Although there is unemployment among teachers, there is still a desperate shortage of specialist teachers – teachers of mathematics, of science, of modern languages, such as French, Spanish, Russian, German, of music, of craft, of religious education. And even if such teachers were easily available, could we be sure that they were of the right calibre for the job of passing on their knowledge to children?

There are enough engineers but not enough competent engineers. Of those admitted to universities to read for engineering degrees, forty-two per cent possessed no better grades at A-level than three Cs (the proportion of students admitted with such comparatively low grades for all other subjects was twenty-nine per cent). In the polytechnics, as many as seventy-two per cent of students admitted for engineering degree courses had nothing better than two A-level D Grades. No wonder that departments of engineering readily admit overseas students. Their entry qualifications are often better than the home-grown variety and they tend to save the departments from total extinction.

This is what Dr John Rae, Headmaster of Westminster School, had to say on the subject[3]: 'If there is a direct connection between the quality of engineers and our industrial performance (and I do not believe that anyone seriously doubts that there is), then these figures should be a cause for concern. It would be a gross over-simplification to put all the blame on the sixth-form curriculum, but it must be a contributory factor, if for no other reason than that by allowing specializing at sixteen it effectively reduces by half the pool of potential engineers. The general example is just as serious. The overwhelming bias in our sixth forms is in favour of what is academic and pure, and against what is practical and applied. At its best the academic sixth form develops fine qualities of intellect; at its worst it encourages a pseudo-intellectual posturing . . . Far too many of our boys and girls leave school not so much ignorant of the industrial world in which they and their country must earn a living as actively hostile to that world.'

Dr Rae, then chairman of the powerful Headmasters' Conference,

3 Writing in *The Sunday Telegraph*, 'Low Levels and A-Levels', 18 September, 1977.

which has more than 200 of the country's top public schools in membership, told delegates attending its annual meeting in Oxford later that same month, that independent schools should have far closer relations with the state sector of education and that their heads should not object to, indeed should even welcome, some control of their institutions by the Secretary of State for Education. It was not a popular statement to make. Some delegates were even shocked at the very idea.

Certainly, it came at a time when independent schools were being threatened from the Left. The direct grant schools were being phased out altogether, and many of them had already decided to go fully independent; boarding schools were finding it increasingly difficult to make ends meet without putting up fees term after term after term (day schools, incidentally, were also being forced to increase fees term by term) and the number of boarders was showing a drop over the past five years. What the Labour Government was failing to achieve (the total annihilation of the independent sector) inflation coupled with the spiralling cost of living seemed to be achieving for them. Or so it seemed momentarily at any rate. The Rae statement was looked upon by some as a gasp of desperation, a death-rattle almost, from the private sector.

It was, of course, nothing of the kind, nor did it need to be. More and more parents – and by no means only those from the upper echelons of society – are seeking to place their children in public schools. True, boarding education, except for those needing it as a result of home background problems (divorce, separation, illness, parents' jobs taking them abroad to places with inadequate educational facilities) is on the decline. Day schools, on the other hand, have never had it so good. Their waiting lists are growing almost as rapidly as their fees are rising.

Why? Because parents are afraid. They fear that their children are not being given a proper start in life, that they will end up leaving school and going straight into unemployment because they have not been properly fitted for any job by their state schools, that they have not been taught how to read properly, or how to write a decent letter of application for a job, or how to solve a reasonably simple mathematical problem.

In fact, we are back full circle, in a sense, to Mr Callaghan's Ruskin speech. Comprehensive schools, even their Labour advocates are admitting, have not turned out to be the panacea for the nation's educational ills. Parents living in poorer districts found schooling particularly bad: rapid teacher turnover (slowed down by the big Houghton pay award for teachers but never actually arrested) did not help matters; there was indiscipline, oversized classes, poor quality teaching, the need for remedial classes in the Three Rs . . . Comprehensives in the better-off, middle-class, green-belt areas fared better – and housing in such areas soon reflected the value of neighbourhood schools in its pricing – and it often became a case of either sending Johnny to a reasonably near public day school or moving to an area known to have a good comprehensive school.

It was strange that the very political party which one had expected to *help* the poorer child, turned out, in fact, to be *hindering* it. Calls for 'equality of opportunity' are all very well in theory (and, indeed, it is a theory worth striving for) but don't always work in practice when society stands divided and when duke and dustman simply do not live in the same street.

And so it came about that Norman St John-Stevas made the pledge in September 1977 that a Tory Government would re-open the direct grant school list, widen and strengthen it and restore to parents whose only wealth is their academically bright children, the right to have them educated in 'centres of excellence' dotted about the country. As chief Opposition spokesman on education he had the full backing of the Shadow Cabinet to make such a promise. It was a valuable election asset.

But what of the 'other side'? After all, it was thanks to Mr Callaghan that there had been a Great Debate on education at all (although, in fairness, such a debate had raged since the production of the first Black Paper on education in 1969 and much of what was being said last year by Labour had been fully discussed already by the Tories and by the so-called Black Paperites and other, similar pressure groups). Well, there *was* a Green Paper.

After all the talk (conferences were conducted in regions up and down the country) one had expected a discussion document that would spell out exactly what Mrs Shirley Williams and her cohort of advisers intended to do. A multitude of reforms had been forecast. The clairvoyants were disappointed. The Green Paper, far from being a statement of intent, turned out to be no more than a kind of commercial break between parts one and two of the ongoing debate.

It made a number of recommendations. If one counted them, there were forty-seven, though not a single one was firm. Each begged a further question and promised still more discussion. So one had, for instance, the recommendation that incompetent teachers should be dismissed or 'moved sideways' – a problem which has bedevilled education for years. Yet there was no real suggestion as to how this would be achieved. The Government would first 'consult' teachers' unions on how this matter should be tackled.

Priority should be given to applicants for teacher training who had already worked outside education since leaving school, the Green Paper said. This would break the traditional 'school-college-school' cycle. But there was nothing hard and fast, nothing 'ordained' about it. Nor was there anything definite about the vexed question of a common core curriculum. Although Mrs Williams would have liked to see schools teaching an 'agreed syllabus' on certain subjects (maths, English language, a science and a foreign language at least) she sidestepped the problem by saying that she had not the power to dictate to schools or local authorities on such matters, nor would she wish to have such powers. More's the pity. Many, if not all heads would, I believe, welcome some outline of curriculum terms of reference from the centre, rather than be left holding a do-it-yourself kit.

Quite separately from the Green Paper was another major talking point: how schools should be governed in the future. After more than two years of deliberations, the Taylor Committee published its report in September 1977, and recommended sweeping changes that would give parents more power in the running of schools than they had ever possessed. One quarter of the places on managing and governing boards should be given up to parents. Pupils should also sit on the boards of secondary schools (a proposal that would require legislation) and all boards should have fewer political representatives, the committee recommended. Indeed, it proposed that every school should have its own, quite separate board, and elections for membership should be school-based.

All sensible suggestions, one should have thought. Certainly, the scrapping of most politically appointed managers and governors is a reform that should be welcomed with fanfares. I have always found this system of running schools a total disaster. For any political party to dictate the running of schools according to which side got in at the local elections, and often place in such positions of power people who know little if anything about education, the school or its pupils and teachers, could only be described as idiotic. It is little wonder that schools were, as a result, turned into ideological footballs to kick from side to side as politics changed.

However, there are also the weaker points of the Taylor report:

it would, for instance, mean that the country's 30,000 or so schools in the state sector, would be administered by as many managing and governing boards. This would mean having to find somewhere in the region of 100,000 people for the jobs. Would all parents, say, at all schools be up to the job of governing them? Would they even be interested in doing so?

Another question mark hanging over Taylor is that concerning the curriculum. The governing boards are expected to decide each school's broad aims and what should be taught in it. Thus, parents *et al* will have to vote on matters such as which reading method the school in question should adopt, or whether it should teach traditional or modern maths. I foresee serious problems on this front, problems that will doubtlessly create friction between teachers and parents.

What other problems face Britain as she approaches the twenty-first century? As a member of the European Community, this island will have to wake up to the fact that the seas have contracted and that our neighbours are nearer than they have ever been. The need for modern languages – and the ability to speak them fluently – is a vital one. It is tragic that languages such as German, Spanish and Russian are being neglected in our schools for the lack of teachers.

It is also a pity that education is being made to suffer all the major cuts during the recent years of recession. Higher Education, in particular, has been trimmed to such an extent that dons are having to neglect research and libraries go without books. Cut education and one cuts the lifeline to the future.

In this introduction, I have tried to summarise what must be considered only a small part of the huge canvas that makes up education in this country. There is, of course, more. Much, much more. This little reference book tries to fill in the vast remainder and answer the kinds of questions I am asked almost daily by scores of anxious parents.

Educationists could spend hours on end speaking in initials and a type of coded jargon. I have tried to decipher much of the code, in alphabetical order and with as many cross-references as possible. Useful addresses have been listed at the back of the book.

I do not pretend that I have covered every permutation of education. To do so would require a book four times as long as this. If I have omitted any organizations, I beg forgiveness. No offence was intended. I ask them to contact me so that they may be included in a future edition, space permitting. But I hope that those who use this book will find it of help.

Finally, let me thank the many organizations, associations and unions which have responded so quickly to my requests for information. My grateful thanks also to my faithful and long-suffering secretary, Ettie Duncan, for her unstinting help and good Scottish humour, and to Maureen, my wife, and Paul my son, who braved the constant noise of typewriter keys and suffered my seclusion with commendable patience. Without them, I could never have written the pages that follow.

John Izbicki

A

Ability Before the introduction of comprehensive education, children were divided into groups according to their particular ability. This meant that they were sent either to grammar schools, secondary modern or technical schools. Within each of these schools, they were also grouped or streamed according to their ability. Some went into A-streams, others into B-streams, etc. Many comprehensive schools still stream pupils in this way, while some others believe in mixing all abilities within the same class. To establish ability, children underwent, and still undergo a number of tests. These include the Intelligence Quotient (IQ) test, the eleven-plus, and assessments of each child made by teachers.

See: Intelligence Quotient (IQ); Streaming.

Abitur The final examination taken by pupils at German grammar schools. It is virtually the same as Britain's former Higher School Certificate and School Certificate combined and it serves as the passport for entry to German universities and teacher training. The length of German schooling differs. Some of the eleven states have a ten-year period between the ages of six and sixteen; others have a nine-year period up to the age of fifteen, although these few will soon be raising the leaving age to sixteen.

See: Baccalauréat; Gymnasium; Higher School Certificate; School Certificate.

Absence A child who does not attend any session (i.e. morning or afternoon) of full-time schooling is deemed to be absent and is so marked on the class register. The number of absences is usually noted in the child's report. Excuses for absence include illness, religious observation and 'other unavoidable causes', such as a funeral or wedding of a close relative. Notes explaining such absences must be sent to the class teacher by the parent. Absence should not be confused with truancy, although a truant child is also absent. School absentee rates might well be high in any one week, but this does not mean that children have been playing truant. One has to differentiate between legitimate absence and truancy.

See: Attendance; Truancy.

Academic Board A board set up within a college to govern its academic affairs. Its membership usually numbers from about a dozen upwards, depending on the size of the college, and is drawn mainly from the teaching staff, heads of departments, etc. Many have one or two student members to allow for student participation. The board nominates members to sit on the more powerful governing body of the college. Such boards were set up following the Weaver Report of 1968 to allow colleges to become more autonomous and to give their academic staff more decision-making powers. Polytechnics also have academic boards.

Further reading: *Government of Colleges of Education* (Department of Education and Science, 1968).

Accidents at School While a child is on school premises or on school business outside school premises (school visits, projects and the like) the teacher is responsible for his safety. Teachers are *in loco parentis* and are expected to act in as reasonable a way towards pupils as the pupils' own parents. The head teacher is responsible for safety precautions on school premises, including the playground. Pupils hurt at school can be compensated if it is proved that there was negligence on the part of the head or staff.

According to the Schools Amending Regulations, published in 1965: 'The premises of the school shall be kept in a proper state of repair, cleanliness and hygiene and adequate arrangements shall be made for the health and safety of the pupils and staff in the case of danger from fire and other causes.'

All teachers should have a reasonable knowledge of first aid and most schools, particularly big comprehensive schools, now have full-time nurses on the premises and a sickroom where pupils hurt in accidents or those who become ill can be treated and may rest. Parents should make sure that their addresses and telephone numbers, both at home and at work, are available to the school (the secretary normally holds this information) so that any accident other than trivial cuts and bruises can be reported at once to one or other of the parents. Teachers should call in a doctor or an ambulance in the event of more serious accidents and, wherever there is any question of possible legal action, should report full details to the head teacher and to their union or association.

The Royal Society for the Prevention of Accidents has a special division dealing with safety education. Most local education authorities contribute funds to this service. It is concerned with cutting down accidents wherever they occur – at home, school, work, on the roads, on land and at sea. It publishes a journal, *Safety Education*, which it distributes among all schools.

Further reading: *Teachers and the Law* by G. R. Barrell (Methuen, 1966).

ACE See Advisory Centre for Education.

Achievement Quotient (AQ) This is a means of expressing a child's achievement in a given subject, e.g. reading or speaking. It is defined as the ratio of the child's achievement age (i.e. the age he gives the impression of being, judged by his achievement in the subject) to his actual or chronological age and is usually expressed as a percentage.

Achievement Test A standardized test in English and mathematics taken by children from eight to twelve years old to find out their skill and knowledge in these and other subjects.

Activism Some educationists believe that a child can only learn properly if his mind and body are constantly active. Activism is the name given to this theory and it has led many schools, particularly primary schools, to encourage pupils to run around, talk and scream as much as they like.

See: Hadow Report.

Activity Method An educational system that allows children to learn through activity and classes to be run on a less desk-bound way. In other words, instead of applying only chalk-and-talk to explain that there are 100 centimetres in a metre, the teacher could ask the children to measure the classroom, so that they really understand what a metre or twenty metres look like.

See: Discovery Method.

Admissions Admission to school is compulsory by law at the age of five and attendance remains compulsory up to the age of sixteen. Under the 1944 Education Act, it is the parent's duty to send his child to school from the age of five and it is the duty of the local education authority to supply the appropriate education for that child. In some exceptional circumstances, children may be kept away from school and given lessons at home or in some other recognized place. Unless special permission to do so is granted by the local authority, and lessons follow properly laid-down guidelines and pass an inspection, the parent is liable to prosecution.

Admission to an institute of further or higher education requires certain minimal academic qualifications, generally reasonable grades in the General Certificate of Education (GCE) at Ordinary (O) and Advanced (A) levels. Universities may stipulate their own requirements and often offer provisional places to candidates conditional on their obtaining particular grades in certain subjects at A-level. Universities often require three A-levels for admission, though grades vary in accordance with the popularity or unpopularity of the subject to be studied. Polytechnics generally require two A-levels and some O-levels, while colleges of education which, at one time, stipulated a minimum of five O-levels, now often require two or even three A-levels.

See: UCCA; University Entrance Requirements.

Adult Education Spare-time education for adults, often gained by attendance of evening classes. Courses and institutes are usually run and financed by local authorities. Universities and voluntary associations also run them. With the increase in leisure time, demand for adult education classes, particularly in non-vocational fields, has increased by leaps and bounds over recent years, with more than one million adults enrolling each year. Due to cuts in public expenditure during the late seventies, many local authorities have been forced to cut down on courses and shut some institutes. Fees are generally low, even when more recent increases have been taken into consideration. More than 100,000 adults attend university extra-mural departments and about 85,000 participate in courses run by the Workers' Educational Association.

For address to contact, see Appendix.

Further reading: *A History of Adult Education in Great Britain* by T. Kelly (Liverpool University Press, 1962).

See: National Institute of Adult Education; Workers' Educational Association.

Advanced Courses Academic courses in further and higher education that lead to qualifications above the standard of the A-level of the General Certificate of Education or the Ordinary National Certificate.

Advanced Level See A-level.

Adventure Playground A playground for children which differs from the conventional small plot with swings, slides and roundabouts in that it provides material with which children can invent their own games and activities: ropes hanging from trees, the shell of a car, dens, pipes and scrap metal bits and pieces from which children can build creations of their own imagination. Some have play-leaders to give advice and help *if* needed. Such playgrounds are gradually being regarded as an essential part of the community.

For address to contact, see Appendix.

Advisory Centre for Education (ACE) An independent, non-profitmaking body which aims to help answer questions and assist with solving educational problems of parents. Founded in 1960, it is now run from premises in London. To date, it has received and answered in the region of 150,000 letters on topics ranging from pre-school, primary, preparatory and independent schools to higher education, evening classes, careers, grants and education for the handicapped. It publishes numerous pamphlets and reports and a useful magazine, *Where?*, the equivalent in educational terms of that other consumer magazine *Which?* (no relation), which is obtainable by subscription.

For address to contact, see Appendix.

Advisory Councils See Central Advisory Councils.

Advisory Teacher A teacher who has been seconded for a limited period of time by a local education authority to give special assistance to the authority's team of school inspectors. Because of their experience and recognized ability, advisory teachers partake in inspections and assist in the administration of schools with particular problems. Many of them are head teachers.

See: Educational Advisers.

Aegrotat A term used in British universities to describe a certificate explaining that a student was too ill to attend an examination. It is given by examiners when they consider that, had the candidate been present, he or she would certainly have passed. The word is the Latin for 'he is ill'.

Agraphia The inability to write words due to brain damage (as opposed to dyslexia – the inability to read words).

See: Aphasia; Dyslexia.

Agreed Syllabus After the 1944 Education Act made religious education compulsory at all schools, each local authority was required to draw up an agreed syllabus – agreed, that is, between the various religious denominations (Churches) and the teachers' associations together with representatives of the local authority. It is the only syllabus that has to be so drawn up or adopted for use in all maintained schools. In 1977, a teacher of religious education was dismissed by the Hertfordshire education authority because he wanted to teach children at a comprehensive school the literal interpretation of the Book of Genesis. This went against the agreed syllabus, which required the stories to be treated as myths and Hebrew legends and preferred to hold to the evolutionary theories of Darwin.

See: Religious Education (RE); Education Act (1944).

Agriculture Apart from a number of schools of agriculture attached to universities, there are a large number of agricultural colleges, farm institutes and horticultural colleges throughout the United Kingdom. The University of Reading also has a college of estate management, which conducts a number of correspondence courses and gives post-qualification training.

The colleges offer qualifications at diploma and certificate level (NDA and NCA), but Ordinary and Higher National Diplomas may also be obtained (OND and HND).

For address to contact, see Appendix.

Further reading: *Report of the Advisory Committee on Agricultural Education*, better known as the Pilkington Committee (HMSO, 1966).

AHM See Association of Headmistresses.

Aided School Voluntary school whose governors or managers are responsible for the maintenance and provision of the building and who decide on the religious education to be given. Most are either Roman Catholic or Anglican.

See: Voluntary Schools.

Aims of Education The philosophy of what education is all about and why it is that we send children to school and provide something called 'education' for ourselves and others has never really been determined, though many have speculated on such aims. From Plato onwards, the general desire has been to broaden the mind through the acquisition of knowledge – not only facts, but what to do with them once one has learned them. With the launching in 1976 by Mr James Callaghan, the Prime Minister, of a national debate on education, the task was set to specify those aims and to set or improve standards in reading, writing and arithmetic, to teach the young more about the world of work, to extend the teaching of science, technology and engineering and to allow parents a voice in what their children are being taught. But it would not be enough merely to teach a child to read without stimulating that child into developing a pleasure in books so that reading does not stop outside school. It is this appetite for further knowledge together with a sense of right and wrong, a moral code of conduct, that might be considered as the goal to aim for in education.

See: Great Debate.

Albemarle Report A report published in 1960 by the Committee for the Youth Service, under the chairmanship of the Countess of Albemarle, to establish how the Youth Service could help young people to be better citizens. The report, which set the age of youth as being between fourteen and twenty, proposed the expansion of the service over a ten-year period. On its recommendation, the Youth Service Development Council was set up to direct the programme and recruit youth leaders, setting salary scales for them. An emergency training college for the leaders was founded at Leicester. The report urged youth to speak unto youth in their own language.

See: Youth Services.

A-level Advanced certificate examination in the General Certificate of Education, generally taken in the sixth form two years after the Ordinary level (O-level) examination. Two or three A-levels are normally needed to enter a higher education establishment for a degree course or other equivalent qualification.

See: Examinations; O-level.

All-age School A school that admits children of all ages, that is from the age of five (the compulsory school starting age) to sixteen-plus. Many such schools used to exist in villages but they have mostly been shut now. Some independent schools still take such a wide age range.

AMA (Assistant Masters' Association) With the NUT, this is one of the oldest teacher unions. Its inaugural meeting was held in 1891 and its aim was to form a professional organization for secondary school teachers (the NUT was still almost exclusively for primary teachers at that time). In 1901 it became the Incorporated Association of Assistant Masters in Secondary Schools, but was popularly referred to as the AMA, a title it has retained. Under the terms of the Trade Union and Labour Relations Act of 1974, it is a trade union, but it retains its corporate status, with professional objectives as its main motivation – the improvement of the status and authority of its members as those of a learned profession and the protection, promotion and development of their professional interests. It has more recently been striving for the establishment of a self-governing professional body representative of *all* teachers and has supported the report of a Government-commissioned working party in 1970, which recommended the establishment of a Teaching Council.

In 1939 the AMA had 12,000 members. Today, it has more than 42,000, most of them in secondary schools, but a fair proportion in middle schools and in primaries. It works closely with the Associations of Headmasters, Headmistresses and Assistant Mistresses within the Joint Four, which has a combined membership of 80,000.

Among its many publications are its journal *The AMA* (published eight times a year with a circulation of 43,000) and its *Guide for Teachers* (1975), which new teachers will find particularly useful.

For address to contact, see Appendix.

See: Joint Four; NUT (National Union of Teachers).

Ancillary or **Auxiliary Staff** A paid helper in a school who is not a qualified or even trained teacher – someone who helps out either inside the classroom (listening to children read, setting up equipment) or outside it (dinner staff, groundsmen, cleaners, laboratory assistants).

Anderson Report The report in 1960 of Sir Colin Anderson's committee which recommended that state scholarships for the study for first degrees should be abolished and replaced by grants from public funds, on condition that the students held two A-levels in the General Certificate of Education. It also proposed the abolition of parental contributions, though it recommended that, as a first stage, there should be a revision of such contributions, allowing forty per cent of students to receive the full grant.

See: Student Grants.

Anson Law The by-law formulated in 1903 by Sir William Anson, the then Parliamentary Secretary of Education, which gave parents the right to withdraw their children from religious education classes at their school and receive religious instruction at a place of their parents' choice.

See: Religious Education; Education Act (1944).

Aphasia The inability to understand the spoken word (as opposed to the written word) due to brain damage.

See: Agraphia; Dyslexia.

Apprenticeship A training scheme lasting a specified period of time, during which the apprentice learns a recognized trade under the tuition and guidance of a qualified expert in that trade. Teachers used once to be trained in this way – by looking at and learning from more experienced colleagues.

Approved Schools See Community Homes.

Aptitude Test An objective test to measure a person's capability to tackle certain tasks or subjects. Such tests have been used with a certain amount of success by careers teachers and advisers in establishing, or at least estimating, a candidate's suitability for a vocation.

See: Careers Advice.

Arbitration The Burnham Committee, which negotiates teachers' salaries, sometimes fails to agree on offers or demands and a stalemate is reached. The Remuneration of Teachers Act, 1965, provided for an independent arbitration body to be set up. This hears the case for both sides (teachers and employers – the local authorities) and makes a recommendation. The Secretary of State is expected to accept these recommendations except in special circumstances, such as the decision of both the House of Commons and the House of Lords to veto the proposals in view of the national economic situation.

See: Burnham Committees; Remuneration of Teachers Acts.

Area Training Organization (ATO) A regional organization responsible for supervising the training of teachers in the region. Usually, ATOs form part of the area university's department of education as well as the college of education. There are eighteen of them. They were first established in 1945 and examine candidates for first teaching qualifications. They are also responsible for in-service training of teachers.

See: In-service Training.

Art Colleges There are more than thirty art colleges in the country, as well as a number that are attached to universities and polytechnics, at which students may follow courses in art (i.e. painting, sculpture, photography, printing and design) leading to the Diploma in Art and Design (Dip.A.D.). There are also eight colleges of Art and Crafts. Courses are generally approved by the Council for National Academic Awards and cover a wide area. Apart from the fields mentioned above, jewellery and industrial design, textile design and printing, fashion, furniture design and making, metal work and ceramics and many others are studied.

See: Diplomas.

Arts Council A body set up by Royal Charter in 1946 to promote appreciation for and execution of the arts, including music, drama, literature, painting, sculpture and ballet. It assists in the promotion of these in schools and adult education.

For addresses to contact, see Appendix.

Assembly The gathering together of pupils at the beginning of the school day in order to hold a corporate act of worship, usually led by the headmaster, but now often conducted by the children themselves. Notices, from football fixtures to the retirement of staff, are also announced at the end of such assemblies. According to the Education Act (1944), all state-maintained and voluntary schools must begin the school day 'with collective worship on the part of all pupils . . . at the school'. But there is a small let-out clause designed for unduly large schools. The two words 'wherever possible' have been interpreted by many heads to mean that assemblies need not be taken too seriously. In fact, many schools would appear to be in breach of the law as a result of some heads' failure to hold religious assemblies at all. Parents have the right to ask for their children to be excused assemblies on religious grounds. Many heads of multi-racial schools and those of humanist persuasions make this multi-racial element into an excuse for non-observance of the law.

See: Education Act (1944); Religious Education.

Assessment of Performance Unit (APU) An organization set up by the Department of Education in 1975 'to promote the develop-ment of methods of assessing and monitoring the achievement of children and to seek to identify the incidence of underachievement'. It has set up working groups on language, mathematics and science and plans also to investigate personal, social, physical and aesthetic development. A special monitoring programme in mathematics is expected to begin in 1978 and in language in 1979. It was formed in 1975 under the head of Mr Brian Kay, who has since been promoted to Chief Inspector (Planning Command). The APU's structure in-volves a co-ordinating group of teachers, local education authority advisers, teacher trainers and HM inspectors, who recommend areas of the curriculum to be investigated, and working groups of similar membership, who decide what aspects of educational performance should be monitored within these areas.

For address to contact, see Appendix.

Assistant Masters' Association See AMA.

Assistant Teacher Any member of staff in a school who teaches, other than the head teacher (also referred to as assistant master or assistant mistress). Assistant teachers are not, as is sometimes supposed, teacher assistants.

Association of Blind and Partially Sighted Teachers and Students (ABAPSTAS) A registered charity founded in 1970 by blind teachers and students to enable the visually handicapped working in education to exchange ideas, pool experiences and in-fluence the development of services designed to meet their needs. It is represented on the executive council of the Royal National Institute for the Blind. It is urging to promote the application of computers to braille production, the development of reading devices, and has helped to ensure the supply of tape recorders, typewriters and braille writing machines to blind teachers.

For address to contact, see Appendix.

Association of Christian Teachers (ACT) An organization

founded in 1971 from an amalgamation of three other organizations – The Teachers' Prayer Fellowship (founded 1926), the Christian Education Fellowship (1947) and the Inter-School Christian Fellowship Teachers' Section (1947). It has nearly 3000 members. Its purpose is to ensure that Christian values and ideals play a significant part in the development of educational theory and practice within society and it is usually well represented on local, regional and national professional groups. Although it is not primarily an organization for teachers of religious education (RE), it has stood at the forefront of the debate on the future of religious teaching in schools. It publishes a journal, *Spectrum*, three times a year (January, May, September).

For address to contact, see Appendix.

Association of European Education Correspondents An organization founded in Holland by John Izbicki in 1976 to bring together the education correspondents of newspapers, journals and the media from the member states of the European Economic Community (Common Market) and to promote better understanding and exchange of ideas within the Market of mutual educational interests and problems.

For address to contact, see Appendix.

See: Education Correspondents Group.

Association of Headmistresses (AHM) Founded in 1874 by Frances Mary Buss (incorporated 1896), the association's members are the headmistresses of recognized secondary schools in both the state-maintained and independent sectors. It aims to support and protect the interests of women engaged in education generally, but particularly in secondary education, to exchange ideas with other heads, governors, managers and other educationists and to exert pressure on Parliament to promote and protect educational matters.

For address to contact, see Appendix.

Association of Headmistresses of Preparatory Schools (AHMPS) Affiliated to the Association of Headmistresses, the association was founded in 1929 to provide an opportunity for the heads of girls' preparatory schools to discuss problems and methods of teaching the curriculum, to meet the heads of senior schools to discuss the children who will be passed on to them and to put forward composite opinions on preparatory education to the Department of Education and Science.

For address to contact, see Appendix.

See: Association of Headmistresses; Preparatory Schools.

Association of University Teachers (AUT) Affiliated to the

TUC in 1976, the association has about 29,000 members comprising all grades of university teachers and administrative, library and research staff. It provides legal advice, offers insurance and a benevolent fund, negotiates salaries and conditions nationally for university teachers and represents generally the voice of the academic. There is an executive committee of twenty-five which reflects all grades and disciplines and five full-time officials with their supporting staff. Each university has its own AUT branch run by honorary officers and committees. There are seventy-six such branches at university institutions.

For address to contact, see Appendix.

Attendance Every parent or guardian has the duty under the 1944 Education Act to cause his child of compulsory school age (i.e. between five and sixteen) to receive a full-time education in accordance with his or her 'age, ability and aptitude'. This does not necessarily mean sending the child to a school in the recognized sense of the term, as long as the child is provided with a *recognized* alternative which also follows a proper curriculum and is full-time.

A local authority also has the duty under the same law to provide a full-time education to every child aged between five and sixteen in its area and is required to admit children to schools at the beginning of the term *after* the age of five has been attained (where sufficient places are available, children are now often admitted at the start of the term immediately before their fifth birthday).

Attendance for a full-time education means being present for lessons throughout the school year. This has been divided into 400 sessions, each morning and afternoon counting as a session – i.e. 200 days a year. Local authorities may deduct up to twenty sessions for occasional vacations during the terms, the year being divided into three such terms (winter, spring and summer, sometimes also known as the Christmas term, Easter term and summer term). The school has to provide a minimum of three hours of secular instruction a day to children aged between five and eight and four hours of such instruction to those aged between eight and sixteen.

Parents who fail to cause their children to attend school (or a recognized alternative place for full-time education) regularly make themselves liable to an attendance order and could be taken to court and fined. Fines range up to £10 and failure to pay can lead to imprisonment, though a judge has the power to impose both a fine and imprisonment. Excuses for non-attendance that are acceptable include illness – in which case the parent is required to send a note to the form teacher explaining the nature of that illness; days of religious observance (in non-denominational schools, or denominational schools attended by children of other faiths, holy days are recognized and Jewish, Moslem, Roman Catholic and children of other religions are allowed to absent themselves legitimately on such days; again, an explanatory note from parents is required); and other 'unavoidable causes'. The latter covers a number of reasons. For example, the child is normally permitted to stay off school if his or her family is celebrating an important anniversary, if a parent or close relative is dangerously ill or if there is a wedding or a funeral of a parent or close member of the family. It is left to the discretion of teachers to permit absence for such occasions and written requests from parents are not unreasonably refused.

See: Absence; Attendance Order; Home Tuition; Truancy.

Attendance Order Such an order is issued by local education authorities if it is considered that a child is failing to attend school in accordance with the law or if he or she is not receiving a proper alternative full-time education. An order, once issued, gives the parent fourteen days in which to satisfy the authority that the child is receiving a proper full-time education. It is up to the parent to prove this and could entail the child's being educated at home or by a private tutor elsewhere to the eventual satisfaction of the authority's inspectors. Parents could (and do) argue that the child has not been registered at the school of their choice and that they will continue to keep the child at home until a place at such a school is made available. The local authority can then appeal to a court and, if the court finds against the parent, a fine or imprisonment or both can be imposed on the responsible parent or guardian. In certain circumstances, the local authority can have the child taken into care – i.e. away from the parent and into a local authority home.

School attendance orders remain in force until revoked or until the child has passed the statutory school leaving age (sixteen).

See: Absence; Attendance.

Audio-visual Aids Equipment that gives help to teachers in classroom lessons by sound (hence audio) or vision. Aids used include radios, televisions, tape recorders, overhead projectors, epidiascopes, gramophone records, slides etc., as well as the long established wall-charts, posters and paintings.

AUT See Association of University Teachers.

Autism A disorder of the mind manifested in children who, though quite bright and even very bright indeed, nevertheless remain withdrawn and sometimes frighteningly aloof, rarely establishing any close relationship with people, even their parents. Autistic children often suffer severe educational retardation, speech defects, poor sight. Such children have often been mistaken for morons and require special education and medical treatment for possible psychoses. They have only comparatively recently been recognized as being in need of such special treatment, and are now being helped to a degree, still insufficient, by a number of voluntary bodies.

For address to contact, see Appendix.

Further reading: *Early Childhood Autism* by J. K. Wing (Pergamon Press, 1967).

See: Dyslexia.

B

B.A. See Degree.

Baccalauréat The French academic examination taken at the end of the grammar (lycée) education, which acts as a virtual passport to university entry. Taken in two parts, at about the age of seventeen or eighteen, it is similar to the German Abitur and the old British Higher School Certificate, although it covers a wider range of subjects.

See: Abitur; School Certificate; Higher School Certificate; Lycée.

BACIE (British Association for Commercial and Industrial Education) Founded in 1919 and registered as an educational charity, it is the only voluntary organization specializing in all aspects of commercial and industrial education and training in Britain. Its members include industrial and commercial firms, the nationalized industries, goverment departments, industrial training boards, local education authorities, universities, technical and commercial colleges, professional bodies, trade associations and trade unions. It produces a wealth of publications from guides on how to write business letters, use of the telephone in business, how to prepare and present talks and lectures, to reports on examinations, industrial training boards and vocational education. It publishes its own monthly *BACIE Journal*.

For address to contact, see Appendix.

Further reading: *A Training Officer's Guide to the Education System of Great Britain*, edited by D. Wheatley (BACIE, 1976).

Backwardness This condition in a pupil can range from slight to very severe but a general definition refers to the child whose classroom attainments fall sharply below those of his peers. It can be measured not only by an IQ test but also by the teacher's observation of the child's verbal, physical and emotional shortcomings. These could be also related to his or her home background, particularly if the child fails to adjust to school surroundings, teachers or other pupils over a reasonably prolonged period. At least ten per cent (about one million) of the school population falls into the category of backwardness, for whom specialized, though not necessarily special education, is necessary. Adjustment can be sought by teaching such children in smaller groups, and by ensuring that they have friends and teachers who genuinely care for them and motivate them. Remedial classes with highly experienced teachers, a curriculum especially designed for the needs of such children, and constant attention are needed here.

Teachers should also beware of dubbing as 'backward' children who merely give this impression but who, in reality, are exceptionally gifted with IQs of 140-plus. In such cases, the child might simply be bored and, because of his or her age, be made to follow lessons that are 'too young' for his or her true ability. Such children could, through insufficient attention being paid to them, turn into serious misfits, disrupters and hooligans.

See: Gifted Child; Intelligence Quotient (IQ); Remedial Classes.

Banding Some local authorities, such as the Inner London Education Authority (ILEA), have tried to improve their comprehensive schools by making sure that their pupil intakes reflect a fair spread of abilities. Primary schools are asked to assess pupils in their fourth year and place them into three groups of 'bands' in verbal reasoning, English and mathematics. The first band contains the above average ability group; the second contains children considered average, and the third those thought to be below average. The ILEA tries to apportion intakes to schools comprising fifty per cent average pupils, twenty-five per cent above average and twenty-five per cent below average.

Basic Staff The minimum number of teaching and non-teaching staff that a school must employ in order to be within the requirements of the local authority in which the school falls. Schools may employ personnel over and beyond their basic staff requirements but must never fall below such allocations.

B.Ed. (Bachelor of Education) A four-year degree course combining both a normal degree course and professional teaching qualification. It can be taken at colleges of education and numerous polytechnics. Certain universities offer the degree at honours level. Under new proposals, a three-year course will entitle the students to a degree at pass level while the fourth year will add the honours level.

Bilateral School A secondary school which combines two school systems, such as a grammar and a technical school.

Bipartite System A description of secondary education as being divided into secondary modern and secondary grammar schools. It is now gradually disappearing with the growth of the all-ability comprehensive school attended by more than eighty per cent of the nation's children of secondary school age.

See: Tripartite System.

Birth Rate Partly because of the increased use of 'the Pill' and other contraceptive devices, the birth rate has been falling rapidly since the early seventies. In 1970, there were 784,000 births; by 1974 there were 640,000 births and in 1976, only 585,000 births. As a result of this steep decline, the Government decided to cut back radically on teacher training by closing or merging many colleges of education, since fewer teachers would be required in schools by 1981 and numerous schools might also have closed by then.

Black Papers A series of books containing articles by teachers, dons, politicians, psychologists and educationists attacking modern trends in education that are seen as harmful to children and students and that are bringing education into disrepute. The first, published in March 1969, attracted a great deal of publicity and was seen as the beginning of a major backlash against progressive education and the growth of comprehensive schools.

One month after the appearance of *Black Paper One*, Mr Edward Short, then Secretary of State for Education and Science in the Labour Government, claimed during a speech to the National Union of Teachers annual conference on 8 April 1969, that the publication had marked 'one of the blackest days for education in the past hundred years'.

The first three Black Papers were co-edited by C. B. Cox, Professor of English Literature at Manchester University, and A. E.

Dyson, Senior Lecturer in English at the University of East Anglia. They also brought into prominence one of the authors, Dr Rhodes Boyson, then headmaster of a big North London boys comprehensive. He is now Conservative MP for Brent North and co-editor with Professor Cox of further Black Papers.

First published by The Critical Quarterly Society, a 'bumper' volume containing the first three books in revised form was produced in 1971 by Davis-Poynter Ltd, Broadwick Street, London W1V 2AH.

See: Comprehensive Education.

Block Grant The grant made annually by the Government to local authorities to help pay for the various public services that it runs. Education takes a major portion of this grant.

See: Rate Support Grant.

Block Practice A method of allowing student teachers to practise teaching in schools for a continuous period of a whole term, rather than for the more usual period of three or four weeks spread over the three-year training course. This method has been rarely applied.

See: Teacher Training, Teaching Practice.

Block Release A system in which people are released by their employers to attend educational courses for up to eighteen weeks a year (any periods exceeding eighteen weeks would technically fall into the category of 'sandwich course'). They could consist of short periods of full-time study at a college of further education together with employment in industry or commerce in between study periods.

See: Sandwich Courses; Day Release.

Boarding Schools Residential schools giving full board and accommodation as well as a full education. Children are normally boarded in a series of houses divided into dormitories or single, double or larger rooms, under a housemaster or housemistress. Many of the country's public schools are boarding schools, although most also take in day pupils – those who learn and eat at school but sleep at home. Nearly three per cent of the school population in England and Wales attends boarding schools, which are usually independent, although there is a comparatively small number of local authority-maintained boarding schools.

Board of Governors/Managers See Governors and Managers, Board of.

Borstals The generic term for Home Office-run residential training establishments for young convicted offenders from the age of fifteen up to the age of twenty-two (inclusive). They originated with the opening of the first establishment of this kind in the village of

Borstal, Kent, in 1908. Young offenders are sent to borstals by sessional or assize courts or by the Court of Criminal Appeal. Some borstals are open and more lenient; others, closed and very strict. On the whole, borstals, which generally give vocational training, are stricter than the old approved schools, now community homes.

See: Community Homes.

British Association for Commercial and Industrial Education See BACIE.

British Federation of Music Festivals There are more than 300 competitive music festivals in Britain and parts of the Commonwealth every year. The Federation acts as a clearing house for information and ideas on festival organization, funding and adjudication. The former Music Teachers' Federation has been incorporated in the Federation. It publishes a Year Book giving full information.

For address to contact, see Appendix.

B.Sc. See Degrees.

Bulge A colloquialism for the rapid increase in the number of children who entered schools as a direct result of the sharp rise in the birth rate immediately after World War II and again from about 1958. Recently, the birth rate began a sharp downward trend.

Bullock Report The report of a Committee of Inquiry under the chairmanship of Sir Alan (now Lord) Bullock, set up by Mrs Margaret Thatcher in 1972 (when she was Secretary of State for Education and Science) to investigate the teaching in schools of reading and the other uses of English. It was published in February 1975 and made 333 recommendations. They included: the regular secondment of teachers to full-time courses lasting anything from one term to a year on reading, language and general English; an increase in the number of such courses; more stringent entry requirements of student teachers, who should show higher competence in reading and language; bigger supply of fiction in school English departments; the supply of language consultants and advisers within schools, particularly those of a multi-racial type; more home-tutoring facilities for immigrant families; the formation of 'reading clinics' and remedial centres in every authority; planned reading programmes for teachers; secondary schools should receive detailed reports on each pupil's reading abilities. The report has become the master-plan for all school English departments, but as was pointed out in a brief foreword by the then Secretary for Education, Mr Reginald Prentice, 'action on those [recommendations] which would involve additional resources must be postponed'.

See: Functional Literacy; Illiteracy.

Bullying This is undoubtedly the nastiest problem that children can experience at school and one which has led to a great deal of misery and even a few tragedies, including suicides by young schoolgirls. Unfortunately, children rarely report the bully for fear of being considered a 'tell-tale' and out of sheer terror that such a report could lead to further bullying. For that reason, bullying is all too rarely discovered. When it is, teachers should stamp on it hard. Parents should be brought in and the bully suspended at once before any further harm is done.

Parents have a responsibility here. If they see evidence that their child has been bullied (reluctance to explain the recurrent bruising or black eye; reticence in talking about schoolmates; frequent bouts of private tears, particularly when alone in bed), they should seek an immediate interview with the child's head teacher and class teacher. If, after careful questioning, the child tells his parents about the bully, the bully's name should be reported to the school at once so that action may be taken.

New children, particularly those recently moved to the area who start school in the middle of a year, are quite often the victims of bullying. Such children should be firmly advised by parents to stand up for themselves and, if hit, to hit back hard. One is reluctant to advise the bullied to become the aggressor, but only by showing that the child can take care of himself and dish out the bully's own medicine will such methods stop. Bullying often leads the victim to feign illness to stay at home. It also leads to truancy through fear of what might be in store for the child at school.

Not all bullying is physical. Much of it, particularly in girls' schools, comprises verbal taunts which can have the same bitterly painful effects.

However, parents should be careful not to confuse bullying with the occasional quarrel or fight. Most children fall out among themselves and indulge in fights as a normal trial of strength. Such occurrences form a normal part of the lesson of life and society and are resolved as quickly as they are begun. Bullying is quite another matter. It is vicious and continuous, usually involves one pupil (who is probably maltreated at home and wants to assert himself or herself) or a small gang led by one such pupil whose prey is either new to the school or weak and inoffensive or, worst of all, mentally or physically handicapped.

See: Truancy.

Burnham Committees A series of committees, founded in 1919 under the chairmanship of Lord Burnham, whose task it is to negotiate and agree salary scales for the various groups of teachers, and to recommend such scales to the Secretary of State for Education and Science. Once the salary structure and scales have been agreed by the Secretary, every local authority is bound to pay them in full but not to exceed them. The committees consist of representatives of the Department of Education, the local education authorities (the employers) and the teachers (employees) under an independent chairman.

Each of the two sides, called panels, has a leader and, to avoid noisy squabbles, only leaders are allowed to address the full committee. For this reason, the committee often separates to permit each panel to discuss claims or offers *in camera* and return with arguments, counter-claims, counter-offers or agreements.

The two main committees are the Burnham Primary and Secondary Committee, which deals with the salaries of teachers, including heads, in schools in these sectors, and the Burnham Further Education Committee, which negotiates salaries for teachers, including principals, at polytechnics, technical colleges and other FE institutes.

Other committees which negotiate salaries include:

Farm Institutes Committee, dealing with salaries of teachers in agricultural institutes and colleges.

Pelham Committee for teachers in colleges of education (teacher training colleges).

Soulbury Committee for salaries of inspectors, organizers and educational advisers, including educational psychologists, employed by local authorities.

Joint Negotiating Committee for youth leaders and community centre wardens.

Burnham Scale Salary structure for teachers, negotiated by a nationally constituted series of committees composed of representatives for teachers and their employers. The scales range in accordance with the qualifications, experience and length of service of the teachers.

See: Burnham Committees.

Bursar The treasurer of a college or independent school who not only runs the financial side of the establishment's administration but who will also give advice to parents or students on fees and other costs. A bursar in a Scottish university or school is a student who holds a scholarship.

Burt, Sir Cyril (1883–1971) He is believed to have been the first person ever to be appointed as a local authority educational psychologist (to the London County Council in 1913), in which capacity he investigated and reported extensively on educationally subnormal children, gifted children and the problems facing London schools. He stayed in this appointment until 1932, then became Professor of Psychology, London. Although a firm geneticist, he believed that poverty, ill-disciplined home background and bad environment could lead to child delinquency and educational backwardness. Under his guidance, educational psychology became respectable. His work on intelligence quotients paved the way to the selective tri-partite school system. Attempts in 1976 to discredit his research methods in a British Sunday newspaper (it accused him of forging or inventing many of his findings) did little if anything to diminish the widely accepted importance of his pioneering work.

See: Educational Psychology; Intelligence Quotient (IQ).

Bussing A method of spreading children of different abilities among schools in separate areas. The word has developed emotive connotations since it is often seen as a method of spreading children according to racial origins. Thus, a local authority which has a predominance of, say, West Indians or Asians in one locality might 'bus' – i.e. transport by school buses – a certain percentage of their 'ghetto' area to schools in another area which is less predominantly coloured. Children from the 'white' area could be similarly bussed to schools in the ghetto catchments. As a result, each school has a fairer share of immigrant children. Clearly controversial, bussing is seen by some as an obnoxious form of racialism; others oppose it because it tends to split friends who live in the same street by sending them to schools that are far apart in distance; others, however, welcome bussing as a realistic method of integrating different races and of preventing schools from being almost exclusively 'black' or 'white'.

Butler, R. A., See Education Act (1944).

C

Capitation Allowance or **Per Capita Allowance** Literally, the 'per head' allowance given annually by local education authorities to schools for the purchase of textbooks, equipment and other materials. Amounts of money are allocated on the basis of the number of pupils in the school and vary with the pupils' ages. Thus a primary school will receive less money per head than a secondary school. Extra allowances are given for sixth forms on the assumption that more advanced work costs more, while little children require only few resources. This theory is often considered to be unjustified.

Careers It would obviously require another book to explain exactly how many careers are open to young people and from how many jobs and professions they can choose. One can do no better than to point out that just such a book exists and to recommend a companion volume to this book: the *Careers A-Z*, which has been compiled by Anne Daniel and Bridget Taylor of the *Daily Telegraph* Careers Information Service, and published by Collins (1975).

There are a number of other useful publications in this field. They include: *Careers Guide* (published annually by the Careers and Occupational Information Centre, HMSO); *Vocational Choice* by M. Smith and P. March (Hobsons Press, for CRAC); *Which Career? A guide for the Undecided* by C. Avent (Robert Hale).

See: Careers Teachers; Careers Advisory Officer; CRAC (Careers Research and Advisory Centre); Careers Advice.

Careers Advice The guidance given to young people concerning what jobs they might best be suited to according to their aptitude, ability and qualifications. This task is generally undertaken by a careers advisory officer, but all too often it is carried out by teachers at school. Some of these teachers have been specially trained in giving careers advice, but many take on the responsibility without any qualifications (it might often be the geography or English teacher, doing the job as a side-line). At present, careers advice is still not sufficiently developed and is often left too late, when the boy or girl is in the final year of school. Lengthy, individual interviews are necessary between student and adviser. The candidate's own preferences, together with a proper assessment of his classroom work, his knowledge, say, of languages or a science, his personality, initiative, staying power, and a host of other considerations must be taken into account, as must the qualifications needed for any particular job in which he is interested and his ability to achieve them.

See: Aptitude Test; CRAC (Careers Research and Advisory Centre); Careers Advisory Officer.

Careers Advisory Officer (CAO) Most local education authorities have a Youth Employment Service which employs CAOs. They advise youngsters, at interviews held at school or college or in their offices, about further or higher education or jobs for which they might be suited. Unfortunately, in many cases such advice is given in the last school year when it is often too late. Some CAOs are now approaching the task of seeing and speaking with future job seekers earlier, while they are still in the fourth or fifth form.

For address to contact, see Appendix.

See: Careers Advice; Careers; Careers Teachers.

Careers Research and Advisory Centre See CRAC.

Careers Teachers Since the raising of the school leaving age there has been an increasing need to teach youngsters about the world of work and to guide them into choosing the right career for themselves. Unfortunately, local authorities have not really planned sufficiently to staff schools with well qualified careers teachers and there are still too few such teachers available. In far too many cases, careers advice is in the hands of teachers whose speciality lies in other subject areas. However, the National Association of Careers Teachers is pressing for more properly trained men and women to staff the careers departments of schools and further education colleges.

For address to contact, see Appendix.

See: Careers; Careers Advice; Careers Advisory Officer; CRAC (Careers Research and Advisory Centre).

CASE (Confederation for the Advancement of State Education) A non-political, non-sectarian confederation of about eighty autonomous local associations. It is voluntary and employs no paid staff, nor does it receive any Government grant. It is concerned with the parental role in education and regularly campaigns for improvement in educational facilities and standards as well as for the greater involvement of parents in education, such as through the membership of education committees and managing and governing bodies. It has always favoured comprehensive education and has been in the forefront of campaigns to end selection for secondary education.

For address to contact and for details of subscription rates, see Appendix.

Further reading: *Parents and Schools*, CASE's regular newsmagazine.

See: Parent-Teacher Associations, National Confederation of; PTA.

Catchment Area See Zoning.

Catholic Teachers' Federation An organization for teachers established in 1907 for the protection of Roman Catholic schools within the community. The federation believes that only Catholic schools can fulfil the demands of Catholic parents. More recently, the federation was in the forefront of the battle to preserve Roman Catholic direct grant schools.

For address to contact, see Appendix.

CATs (Colleges of Advanced Technology) See Universities; Robbins Report.

Central Advisory Councils Two such councils – one for England and one for Wales – were set up in 1944 to advise the Secretary of State for Education and Science (then the Minister of Education) on any educational matters, whether in theory or practice. They have met rarely – the last time being the meeting of the English council in 1967, which produced the famous Plowden Report. At the 1977 North of England Education Conference, Mrs Shirley Williams, Education Secretary, was urged to convene the councils again to advise on current educational problems.

See: Plowden Report.

Central Register and Clearing House Ltd Like the UCCA clearing house, this body was set up to assist candidates who wish to become teachers to enter colleges of education or polytechnics. Each candidate is first considered for admission by the institution placed first in the list of preferences on the completed form. If the institution concerned cannot accept the candidate, the application is then passed by the Central Register to the second institution listed, and so on if necessary.

For address to contact, see Appendix.

See: Clearing House; UCCA.

Centre for Educational Disadvantage An independent information centre concerned with giving advice on the teaching methods, curriculum and other special needs relevant to the education of disadvantaged children and immigrants. It was set up following the publication of a White Paper in 1974 on *Educational Disadvantage and the Educational Needs of Immigrants*. In July 1975, the Secretary of State for Education appointed a governing body for the centre and its chairman, Sir Alec Clegg, former chief education officer of the West Riding of Yorkshire. The Centre's headquarters opened in September 1976 in Manchester. It is funded by the Department of Education, but does not fall under its direction.

For address to contact, see Appendix.

Certificate of Education Examination qualification proposed by the Schools Council in 1976 to replace both the O-level examination of the General Certificate of Education and the Certificate of Secondary Education at the age of sixteen-plus. The Council and its working parties felt that with the rapid development of comprehensive education, pupils at this age should be given the opportunity of sitting a single system of examination, which would be graded in such a way as to give both high and low ability children a chance. Like the CSE, it was to be controlled both by teachers and external examiners (see Modes 1–3). Although recommended by the General Council of the Schools Council, it faced opposition from employers, universities and a number of teacher organizations, mainly on the grounds that it was likely to be insufficiently testing for high ability candidates and could be found too difficult for the lower ability groups. Many saw the proposed change as a lowering of standards; others, as placing too much power in the hands of the teachers. In 1976, the Education Secretary postponed a decision on allowing the new examination to be introduced by 1981 until more research and feasibility studies had been carried out.

See: Examinations; Schools Council.

Certificate of Secondary Education (CSE) See Examinations.
Certificate of Sixth Year Studies See Education in Scotland (Examinations).
Chancellor The titular head of a university, usually an honorary position held by senior dignitaries of the land or members of the Royal Family. The Chancellor of Bradford University is Sir Harold Wilson; that of Keele University is Princess Margaret; of London University, the Queen Mother; of Manchester, the Duke of Devonshire; of Salford, Prince Philip; of Wales, Prince Charles.
Chief Education Officer A permanent, paid official who acts as the chief administrative officer of a local education authority. Although theoretically the servant of the politically elected education committee, he acts as their adviser and, together with his assistants and a (generally) large staff of other local civil servants, rules over the authority's educational establishments and staffs. He is sometimes called the authority's Director of Education or, as in the case of the Inner London Education Authority, more simply the Education Officer.
Childminding Up to 200,000 children under the age of five are cared for during the day by childminders. The figure could be higher. There is no precise idea of how many children are being looked after in this way or, indeed, how many childminders there are. One

only knows for certain of some 60,000 children in the daily care of childminders who have registered with the local authorities as such. The service has grown rapidly in recent years. As no qualifications are needed (an error that ought to be rectified), just about anyone can take in toddlers. In the absence of universal nursery provision, and with the rise in the number of working women and one-parent families, the need for the childminder has grown with equal rapidity. Some women, it has been established, have taken in young children because they themselves have had to give up work through bad health – not the best way to start looking after very young children, many of them babies. Some minders take in far more children than there is room for. Often they are dumped in a small room, without facilities and rarely played with (sometimes even rarely fed!). There are many other minders, however, who provide an excellent service. Most of these are registered.

Further reading: *Minder, Mother and Child* by B. Mayall and P. Petrie (University of London Institute of Education, 1977); *Childminding* by B. Jackson (in *Low Cost Day Provision for Under-Fives*, Department of Health and Social Security and Department of Education and Science, 1976); *Childminder's Charter* (National Union of Public Employees, 1975).

Children's Rights Workshop An organization which is compiling a register of parents and groups of families who have decided to educate their children at home. For further information, contact address in Appendix.

See: Home Teaching; Home Tuition; Parents' National Education Union.

Christian Education Movement An organization born in 1965 out of the Institute of Christian Education and the Student Christian Movement. It has about 10,000 members and aims to look at schools and the education given in them through the eyes of Christianity. It offers support to all its Christian teacher members, particularly those concerned with religious education. It has published many pamphlets and booklets on controversial topics (drugs, violence, family planning) as well as on other less controversial but equally important issues (conservation, Christmas, housing).

For address to contact, see Appendix.

Church Schools See Voluntary Schools.

Circulars These are memoranda sent by the Secretary of State for Education and Science to local education authorities and/or other interested parties to explain policies or statutory regulations.

They are not laws, but generally imply that, if they are not followed, legally binding regulations may follow. Perhaps two of the most famous or notorious circulars were that issued by a Labour Government in 1965 (Circular 10/65) and that issued by a Conservative Government in 1970 (Circular 10/70). The first requested all local authorities to prepare their plans for the reorganization of secondary schools in their area so that they could all become comprehensive schools. The second scrapped the request in the earlier circular and allowed local authorities to organize their educational provision as they thought best for the children of their area.

See: Regulations.

City and Guilds of London Institute A national body for the advancement of technical and scientific education, founded in 1878 and given a Royal Charter twenty-two years later. Its examinations are designed for industrial workers who wish to add to their industrial experience by attending part-time classes at local technical or further education colleges. More than 250 subjects are covered by examinations for workers in such fields as building, agriculture, electrical engineering, food and catering trades, paper and printing, shipbuilding, motor manufacturing, handicraft teaching and chemical industries.

For address to contact, see Appendix.

Civic Universities Unlike Oxford and Cambridge, the civic universities were not formed on a collegiate system but were set up as colleges of higher education in the city they served. The first was in Manchester in 1851 and was called Owen's College. Today, it is Manchester University. The College of Science in Leeds came second in 1874 – it is now Leeds University. Others in cities throughout the country rapidly followed. At first, they offered only courses for degrees taken externally from London University, and many of them were not given Royal Charters, allowing them full university status and autonomy, until after 1945. Some others, like Birmingham (1900), were given independence earlier.

See: Universities.

Classes, Size of School classes divide the number of children admitted to that school into smaller components. Each component may then be further divided into still smaller sets or groups. Children may be 'streamed' in accordance with their abilities, so that an intake of 120 children of varying abilities might be placed in four classes, each with thirty children, ranging from the high ability group (which might be called the A-stream, Class A or Form 1A) to the least able

(Form 1D). Nowadays, in order to make children believe that they are all equal, classes are no longer graded A–D, but are given a haphazard choice of letters, often the initial of the form teacher's surname. So Mr Robert's class might be 1R and Miss Hopkinson's class 1H. But children soon know which is the top and which is the bottom, if they are indeed streamed classes.

Class sizes differ. A remedial class might have only five pupils while a high ability class thirty-five. Teaching unions want all classes (except remedial classes, which should always be very small) to have a maximum of thirty pupils. So far, primary school classes still seem to have the most (forty and sometimes more) and secondary classes thirty, thirty-five and sometimes, but seldom, more.

See: Regulations; Remedial Classes; Setting; Streaming.

Clearing House A central body which acts as an agency to sort out applications from students and assess their qualifications for entry to universities (or, for teachers, colleges of education) in accordance with places that are available at those institutions.

See: Central Register and Clearing House Ltd; UCCA.

CNAA See Council for National Academic Awards.

Coaching Special tuition usually given privately to an individual child by a teacher at home or in the teacher's home for a fee in order to enable the pupil to improve his or her skill in a particular subject or subjects. Coaching is often given in examination subjects before the pupil has to sit the examination (Common Entrance, GCE O-level or A-level, etc.).

See: Crammer School.

Co-education The education of boys and girls together in the same school or other institution. Britain is now virtually alone in segregating the sexes, although even a number of traditionally single sex public schools are now admitting members of the opposite sex as an 'experiment', albeit only (with certain exceptions) into the sixth form. Opponents of co-education see a danger in the mix of the sexes, lest it should lead to immoral behaviour. The same opponents appear to accept 'mixed' primary schools and 'mixed' universities. It is the in-between secondary phase that causes concern. It is true that girls tend to mature earlier than boys, and some adolescents might undergo brief emotional disturbances as a consequence of being close to the opposite sex. Generally, however, the natural mix of the sexes throughout education appears to cause no harm and could be of considerable advantage. Most state-maintained secondary schools are now co-educational.

Further reading: *Mixed or Single Sex School?* by R. R. Dale (Routledge and Kegan Paul, 1969).

Colleges of Advanced Technology (CATs) See Universities; Robbins Report.

Colleges of Education Formerly known as teacher training colleges, these are institutions where students are trained to become teachers. Until now, minimum entry qualifications comprised five O-levels at GCE, although many colleges demanded at least one A-level as well. Three-year courses led to the Certificate of Education which qualified the student for teaching.

After 1983 only graduates will be allowed to enter the teaching profession and the non-graduate Certificate will gradually be phased out and end altogether after the 1979–80 intake to colleges. From he autumn of 1980, all students entering initial teacher training must have at least two A-level GCE passes. This decision, taken in July, 1977, will ensure that teaching will eventually become an all-graduate profession.

Because of the falling birthrate, coupled with a cut-back in educational spending, the late Seventies saw more teachers emerging from colleges than were required in the schools. Teacher unemployment rose as a result and the Government decided to cut back teacher training places and colleges of education drastically.

In 1972 there were 162 colleges in England and Wales. Many of them ran the four-year course leading to a Bachelor of Education (B.Ed.) degree, as well as in-service courses for practising teachers. Some also ran courses for the Advanced Diploma in Educational Studies and there were (and still are) those that specialize in certain subjects, such as music, arts and crafts, physical education (PE), the teaching of backward or maladjusted children, religious studies, cookery etc.

But by 1981 the number of colleges is to be reduced to a mere eighty.

This move is to be achieved by mergers or amalgamations of colleges with other colleges or polytechnics or universities and the closures of a number of colleges altogether. As many as forty-two closures were announced since 1975.

As a result, the number of training places is also to be radically reduced in order to cope with the falling birthrate, which was expected to drop by as many as 1,600,000 between 1975 and 1985.

It had been planned to train 84,800 teachers in 1981. This figure was cut back (in 1977) by almost half – to 46,670 in England and

Wales. Of these, about 10,000 places were to be reserved for in-service training. It means, therefore, that only about 45,000 teachers will be trained in 1981 – and that all of them will become full degree-holding graduates.

See: Education Cuts.

Common Entrance Examination See Examinations.

Community Homes The new name given to the old approved schools, presumably to induce the idea that they are more like 'home'. Certainly, many of them do have the appearance more of luxury holiday camps than of the correctional establishments they are meant to be. A community home is a boarding school, approved by the Home Secretary, for young people who have been found guilty of an offence by a court of law and have been directed to such a home for care and protection. Since the Children and Young Persons' Act, 1969, these homes have the option of refusing admission to any young person considered to be too ill-disciplined to be controlled. The homes are run like schools, and teach the inmates (aged fifteen-plus) a trade as well as various other subjects.

Further reading: *Children in Trouble* (Cmnd 3601, Home Office, HMSO, 1968); *The New Law of Education* by G. Taylor and J. B. Saunders (Butterworth, 1971).

Community Schools It was the Plowden Report which proposed the setting up of such schools in all areas, but particularly in the educational priority areas, in order to involve not only children but the entire community in creative activities. The schools – a few already exist in various parts of the country – keep open beyond normal school hours and admit parents and others within the community to make use of facilities, such as classrooms, halls, gymnasiums and swimming pools, if any. Meetings of societies and productions by local dramatic and operatic companies may take place within these schools. There are many schools of this type in the United States.

See: Educational Priority Area; Plowden Report.

Compensatory Education A system of channelling more resources into the schools of particularly deprived inner city areas. In order to help socially deprived children obtain a better education, the government introduced special education and welfare programmes in 1968, giving such inner city areas better buildings, equipment and teachers than the average area could expect. Critics believe that the money would be better spent on providing such areas with better housing and conditions.

See: Educational Priority Area; Positive Discrimination.

Complaints Parents are often faced with the problem: to whom do I turn to complain about my son's or daughter's school, teacher, textbooks, homework, detentions, punishments and the like? The list can stretch to inordinate lengths. There are a number of ways in which a parent may proceed with a complaint, depending on its category.

If the question concerns his child's lessons, homework (too much, too little), an individual teacher, a school bully, punishments, etc., the parent should in the first instance turn to the child's teacher, *by appointment*. A quiet talk will often settle matters quickly and amicably. If, however, the parent fails to obtain a reasonable response from the teacher, the next step should be to the head teacher of the school (others might advise first seeing the housemaster or head of year; however, experience suggests that, having already gone to the individual teacher concerned and failed to succeed, one should then turn to the very top). It is likely that the head will call in the teacher to be present at any discussion of a complaint.

Should this, too, fail, a strongly-worded letter should be written to the school's chairman of governors or managers, citing the complaint and pointing out that two interviews (with teacher and head teacher) had been to no avail. The problem is then likely to come before the next meeting of governors/managers. It is unlikely that the parent will need to go any further.

If the complaint is against the school in general or concerns an allegation of a serious nature (e.g. of sexual assault by a teacher on a pupil) it should be made to the chief education officer of the authority under whose jurisdiction the school falls. The police could also be approached in the case of a complaint of a case in law.

Should the complaint be against the local authority itself, (such as the authority's failure to provide adequate schooling facilities, its refusal to give proper choice of schools to the parent, its dictatorial attitudes to secondary reorganization without consultation with the electorate and so on) there are a number of ways in which the parent may make it:

1. To the local MP (but make sure first on whose side that MP happens to be, if the complaint is of a party political or ideological nature!).

2. To the Press. Never be afraid to contact your local newspaper or a national newspaper if you consider the complaint merits national coverage.

3. To the Leader of the (local) Opposition (in the case of a political issue, where an approach to the party in power might be useless).

4. If there are sufficient parents all making the same complaint, get together and march as a body to the local education offices and demand to speak to: the chief education officer (he will probably send down his deputy or assistant chief in the first instance); the chairman of the education committee (this should be done on days when the education committee is meeting, in which case the delegation could lobby the entire committee) and whoever else is considered appropriately concerned.

In the case of the reorganization of a school (from grammar or secondary modern to comprehensive; from single sex to co-educational), it is the duty of the local authority to publish a proper notice to this effect under Section 13 of the 1944 Education Act. The notice must spell out exactly what changes are to be made to the character of the school. Section 13 notices have to be posted conspicuously on or close to the front door of the school concerned and must be published in at least one local newspaper. Once this notice has been published, objections to the plan may be sent by ten or more local electors direct to the Secretary of State at the Department of Education. This must be done *within two months* of the date of publication of the notice. (Incidentally, electors wishing to support plans detailed in a Section 13 notice may also send letters and petitions to the Secretary of State.)

If the complaint concerns the local authority's apparent un-reasonableness in, say, not permitting a child to attend a school of the parents' choice, then the parent may again complain direct to the Secretary of State under Section 68 of the 1944 Act. This allows the Secretary of State to intervene in any case where the authority or the school's governors/managers 'have acted or are proposing to act unreasonably'.

Again, the local and national Press may be contacted by parents. Newspapers generally are excellent watchdogs and will, if they consider the complaint to be a matter of real concern, publicize it in the public interest.

Further reading: *Teachers and the Law* by G. R. Barrell (Methuen, 1966).

Comprehensive Education Education given to children of all abilities in secondary schools which incorporate the tripartite system (grammar, secondary modern and technical schools). By 1977 there were nearly 3 million pupils in over 3000 comprehensive schools, covering about seventy per cent of the secondary school population. Children are not selected for these schools and the system, begun in earnest in 1965, gradually replaced the selection system based on the eleven-plus test.

Comprehensive schools vary in size and are often the amalgamation of two, three or four schools in the same area, thus covering more than one site. They can be organized along various lines: the all-through school, taking children from the age of eleven to eighteen; the two-tier school which takes children aged eleven-plus from their primary school and places them in the junior section of the comprehensive, transferring them at the age of thirteen or fourteen to its senior section; the eleven–sixteen school, which transfers pupils at the age of sixteen-plus to a sixth form college; the middle school system, where pupils stay at primary school until the age of eight or nine and are then moved to comprehensive middle schools until the age of twelve or thirteen, after which they go to the senior or upper school. There are various combinations of the above variety of systems.

Further reading: *The Comprehensive School* by R. Pedley (Penguin, 1969); *Comprehensive Planning, Symposium*, edited by S. Maclure (Councils and Education Press, 1965); *Inside Comprehensive Schools* by T. Burgess (HMSO, 1970); *A Guide to English Schools* by T. Burgess (Penguin, 1969); *The Black Papers*, edited by C. B. Cox and A. E. Dyson (Critical Quarterly Review, 1969 onwards) and by C. B. Cox and R. Boyson (1975 onwards); *Grammar School Tradition in a Comprehensive World* by J. N. Hewitson (Routledge & Kegan Paul, 1969).

See: Circulars; Education Acts (1976 Education Act); Sixth Form College.

Confederation for the Advancement of State Education See CASE.

Confidential Records See School Records.

Confiscation Teachers are usually quick to confiscate any article in the possession of a pupil which they consider to be offensive or a distraction during lessons. Articles could include anything from a stick of chewing gum to a pornographic book or picture. It is the teacher's right to remove such articles promptly and to admonish or otherwise punish the pupil who caused the article to be introduced into the class. However, it is *not* the teacher's right to dispose of the article by its destruction or to damage it or to keep it beyond any reasonable time. Reasonable time can be interpreted as ranging from a day to a term. Usually, it would be wise to return the article at the end of the school day with a warning never to bring it into the class again. Since the article, however offensive, remains the property of the pupil concerned, it cannot be removed from him permanently. Punishment, even instant suspension, may be ordered. But confiscation can only be temporary. If the article is one likely to cause a disruption or wound (a knife or other dangerous weapon) or if it is of such a nature as to be considered a corrupting influence on other pupils, a teacher would be fully justified in confiscating it and then calling in the pupil's parents – to whom the article may then be returned. What they then do with it is up to them.

Consortia There are a growing number of local authorities who have agreed, with the consent of the Department of Education and Science and the Department of the Environment, to form consortia for the design and building of schools and school furniture. Such co-operation has often turned out to save money since materials can be bought in greater bulk and a smaller administrative, architectural and design team can be employed. The consortia are:

CLASP (Consortium of Local Authorities Special Programme), formed in 1957 on the initiative of Nottinghamshire education authority. It involves such members as Bath and Cambridge universities, Coventry, Derbyshire, Durham, Manchester, Nottinghamshire and several other authorities.

SCOLA (Second Consortium of Local Authorities), formed in 1961 following the success of CLASP.

CLEAPSE (Consortium of Local Education Authorities for the Provision of Science Equipment), formed in 1963. Many authorities in the Home Counties are members.

Consortium of Method Building, formed in 1963. Its members include Berkshire, Cornwall, Devon, Oxfordshire, Somerset, and Wiltshire. It allows the designer more freedom in architectural lay-out than the others.

CLAW (Consortium Local Authorities, Wales), formed in 1962. Its members are all Welsh authorities.

CFG (Counties Furniture Group), which draws on the experience of teachers to help design classroom furniture.

For addresses to contact, see Appendix.

Core Curriculum Subjects that form – or should form – the most important part of a student's learning. At school, these could comprise reading, writing and arithmetic at primary level or a combination of subjects across the various disciplines at secondary level, such as English language, a science subject and a foreign language. Although opinions vary as to what should be contained in a core curriculum, there appears to be general agreement that literacy, oracy and mathematics should be among the major components.

Corporal Punishment Physical punishment on the body, usually interpreted as being inflicted by a cane on the hands or buttocks. Although associated with public schools, this form of punishment is practised in state-maintained schools as well.

Teachers are permitted by law to punish children in this way, although the practice is now rarer than in the past and some local education authorities have banned it from primary schools. Each school is obliged to keep a punishment book with a record of each corporal chastisement. Only the head teacher or his/her deputy is supposed to carry out the punishment. Since teachers are, by law, *in loco parentis*, they are allowed to do what any 'reasonable parent' is expected to do to his/her own child. Any other form of beating, such as slaps across the face or about the head, is illegal and teachers who inflict punishment considered irregular or sadistic could face prosecution in the courts for assault. Many schools keep the cane only as an 'ultimate deterrent'.

Further reading: *A Last Resort? – Corporal Punishment in Schools,* edited by P. Newell (Penguin Education, 1972); *Discipline in Schools,* edited by L. Stenhouse (Pergamon Press, 1967); *Discipline in Schools,* edited by B. Turner (Ward Lock, 1973); *Teachers and the Law* by G. R. Barrell (Methuen, 1966); *A Survey of Rewards and Punishments in Schools* by M. E. Highfield and A. Pinsent, National Foundation for Educational Research (Newnes, 1952).

See: Punishment; Society of Teachers Opposed to Physical Punishment.

Correspondence Colleges There are scores of schools and colleges that teach students by correspondence, but only thirty-four are accredited by the Council for the Accreditation of Correspondence Colleges. Generally, students are sent lessons and tests through the post, are told what textbooks to use, and have their work marked by a tutor assigned to them. Examinations, such as O and A-levels as well as university degrees, can be taken as a result of such courses, as can a number of professional qualifications ranging from pilots' and navigators' licences to postgraduate medical and nursing diplomas. By far the biggest in the group is the Open University which links its courses with radio and television programmes, a summer school and tutorials at numerous regional centres. For addresses of other well known colleges, see Appendix.

See: National Extension College; Open University; Parents' National Educational Union.

Council for National Academic Awards (CNAA) A body which was granted a Royal Charter in 1964 following recommendations to set it up contained in the Robbins Report published in the previous year. It validates and awards degrees at non-university institutions, such as polytechnics. These degrees, both first and higher degrees, including the Ph.D., are of the same standing and standard as those awarded by the universities. Degree courses have to be fully approved by the council, which inspects the institutions wishing to teach such courses and satisfies itself with the standards and qualifications of the staff as well as with the general conditions, examinations and facilities offered.

The CNAA has a governing council under a chairman and twenty-one members drawn from the universities, institutes of further education, local authorities and industry and commerce.

For address to contact, see Appendix.

Counselling Most comprehensive schools have teachers on their staffs who act as personal tutors and advisers, while some make use of roving counsellors employed by local authorities to visit schools within the area. They help pupils with personal problems, whether they be academic or emotional, at school or in the home. The counsellor often acts as a 'father confessor' figure to whom the individual pupil may turn for help and advice. Some schools put aside periods on the timetable specifically for group counselling. Pupils may discuss courses and course options as well as careers with their counsellors.

Further reading: *The Faith of the Counsellors* by P. Halmos (Constable, 1965); *Theories of Counselling* by B. Steffire and others (McGraw-Hill, New York, 1965).

CRAC (Careers Research and Advisory Centre) A body founded with a staff of three in 1963 to act as a link between education and industry and commerce, and to develop careers work in schools, colleges and universities. Today it has a staff of eighty and has established, together with Hatfield Polytechnic, the National Institute for Careers Education and Counselling, which helps to disseminate important research details on careers and counselling work. It is a non-profitmaking body and publishes a large number of books and pamphlets with Hobsons Press (Cambridge).

For address to contact, see Appendix.

Further reading: *Annual Register of Research in Guidance and Counselling*; *British Journal of Guidance and Counselling*; *Degree Course Guide*; *Directory of Further Education*; *Practical Approaches to Careers Education* by C. Avent (all published by Hobsons Press); *Careers A-Z* by A. Daniel and B. Taylor (*Daily Telegraph*/Collins, 1975).

See: Careers.

Crammer School This is usually a special school which prepares pupils or students for examinations on a fee-paying basis. The very word 'crammer' suggests that pupils will not so much learn a subject or subjects as be stuffed with the necessary facts, which they will have to commit to memory, to pass the examination concerned.

See: Coaching.

Crowther Report The report in 1959 from the Central Advisory Council for Education under the chairmanship of Sir Geoffrey Crowther on the age-group sixteen to eighteen. It recommended the raising of the leaving age to sixteen between 1966 and 1969 and proposed that the three leaving dates be cut to only two – allowing children to leave school only at Easter or at the end of the summer term. It also attacked the habit of sixth forms to over-specialize and urged the introduction of county colleges and the expansion of block release courses allowing for better vocational training.

See: School Leaving Age.

CSE (Certificate of Secondary Education) See Examinations.

Curriculum A fixed series of studies planned for students to give them the education they are believed to require for their development. Examinations are often taken in subjects contained in the curriculum, but a curriculum may also contain non-examinable subjects to broaden the mind and to develop not only the intellect but also the emotions and social behaviour and understanding of persons. Curriculum development is in the hands of the Schools Council.

See: Core Curriculum; Schools Council.

D

Day Nursery A place, generally run by local authority social services sections, where working parents may leave their children aged under five for the day. In the case of hospitalized children, day nurseries are often attached to hospitals and run by the health authority of the area.

See: Nursery Class; Nursery School.

Day Release A system in which people are released from their employment for one or two days a week to attend educational courses. These are generally part-time vocational courses or courses preparing the student for examinations.

See: Block Release; Sandwich Courses.

Degree A qualification awarded after successfully completing a course in higher education, usually at a university or a polytechnic or similar institution. A degree course normally takes three years in this country, but takes longer (anything from four to seven years) at universities elsewhere in Europe. There are various types of degree, e.g.

B.A. (Bachelor of Arts), a degree in the arts (in Scotland it is the M.A.) such as in English, history, modern languages.

B.Sc. (Bachelor of Science), a degree in the sciences, such as physics, chemistry, mathematics.

B.Ed. (Bachelor of Education), a degree taken after a four-year course at colleges of education and other higher education institutes or departments of education at certain universities. It is a comparatively new degree, suggested by the Robbins Report on higher education in 1963.

All the above are first degrees and most of them are classified as follows:

General Degree, the study of several subjects to degree level.

Honours Degree, the study of one subject in depth or with a second, or subsidiary subject.

Pass Degree, a degree similar to a general degree, requiring the study of several subjects. It can also be a pass grade, the lowest grade in honours.

Honours degrees are graded from first class honours, the highest of the divisions, upper second (or second class, division 1), lower second (or second class, division 2), third class, to pass. Oxford has an additional fourth division.

Oxford and Cambridge universities as well as some of the more recently established universities award only the B.A. as a first degree. There are also a number of specialized Bachelor courses which lead to the B.Lit. (Bachelor of Literature), B.Phil. (Bachelor of Philosophy), B.Mus. (Bachelor of Music), B.Com. (Bachelor of Commerce), LL.B. (Bachelor of Laws).

For medicine, the course can be as long as seven years. A training course lasting five years must be taken at one of the medical schools of a university; once qualified, the young doctor must spend at least a further eighteen months on the staff of a hospital, often one of the teaching hospitals. The first degree for a doctor is the M.B. (Bachelor of Medicine).

Higher Degrees or **Postgraduate Degrees** take the form of higher diplomas, the M.A. (Master of Arts), M.Sc. (Master of Science) or the doctorates, Ph.D. (Doctor of Philosophy), D.Sc. (Doctor of Science), D.Phil. (another form of Doctor of Philosophy), D.Lit. (Doctor of Literature), etc. Usually, the M.A. and M.Sc. are conferred after an additional year's study, research and/or examination (not needed at Oxford or Cambridge, where the Master's degree is given after a lapse of time and the payment of a fee). The Ph.D. and other variants usually follow the acceptance of a previously agreed thesis of considerable length and scholarship.

Honorary Degrees can be conferred by universities and polytechnics on persons who have distinguished themselves in one field or another. They might be musicians, writers or statesmen. No examination is involved and the degree is purely an honour.

Degrees awarded by a university are in the name of the university. Those taken at polytechnics are awarded by the Council for National Academic Awards.

See: Council for National Academic Awards; Diplomas.

Degree Course Guides These are a series of booklets covering all the major degree subjects available at universities and polytechnics. Each booklet looks at the similarities and differences between the universities' courses, entrance requirements, methods of teaching and examining, optional subjects offered, etc. It is published by Hobsons Press for CRAC.

See: CRAC.

Denominational Associations Although the vast majority of schools fall under the jurisdiction of local education authorities and the Department of Education and Science, separate boards still supervise the country's denominational schools, particularly the voluntary controlled, voluntary aided and special agreement schools. These are:

Church of England Board of Education, which has almost fifty diocesan directors of religious education spread throughout the country. See address in Appendix.

The Catholic Education Council, which has numerous representatives in the dioceses. The council also has representatives to deal specifically with colleges of education, universities, and a national Religious Inspector. See address in Appendix.

The Free Church Federal Council Education Committee, which is well represented by local committees. See Appendix for address and list of organizations affiliated to the Federal Council.

Central Joint Education Policy Committee, an inter-denominational body with representatives from the Anglican, Roman Catholic and Free churches. See addresses in Appendix.

Jewish and Quaker education are also supervised by central councils, whose addresses are in the Appendix.

See: Jewish Lecture Committee; Quaker Schools; Voluntary Schools.

Dental Inspections All state-maintained schools must provide facilities for regular dental inspections and treatment. The latter (if minor) may be given on school premises or the pupil may be asked to attend a dental clinic. Parents must be informed of any treatment to be given and have the right to opt for it to be carried out by their own dentist, whether privately or on the National Health Service.

See: Medical Inspection.

DES (Department of Education and Science) The Government department responsible for the entire education system in England as well as for science, libraries and the arts. It is also responsible for post-school education in Wales. (Primary and secondary Welsh education fall under the Secretary of State for Wales, while Scottish education comes under the aegis of the Secretary of State for Scotland.) It was not until April 1964 that the DES was established in its present form. Before that date, it was the Ministry of Education with a Minister at its head, and from 1900 until 1944, when the Education Act on which the present system is based was passed, education came under the Board of Education with a President at the top.

The Department deals with the entire area of education, including primary and secondary schools, universities, teachers and lecturers, further education, teacher training, educational curricula and standards. It has a Secretary of State at its head, who is supported by two Ministers of State, one of whom is Minister for the Arts, and one under-Secretary of State. Its senior official is the Permanent Secretary and there are a number of Deputy Secretaries who are in charge of several branches, each dealing with different aspects of the education system.

The DES controls the broad allocation of resources for education and the rate and distribution of educational buildings. But it does not *run* schools or colleges and has little if any control over the content of education or teaching methods.

It acts within the framework of estimates approved by Parliament and spends only a comparatively small part of the total public expenditure on education. About eighty-five per cent of the total expenditure comes from local authorities, of which some sixty-five per cent is recovered by the authorities from the Exchequer by way of the rate support grant. The balance comes out of local rates.

For address to contact, see Appendix.

Further reading: *How the DES is Organized* – a booklet issued by the DES (updated twice yearly); for a full list of branches and officials' names, titles, etc., see *Education Committees Year Book*, published annually by Councils and Education Press (address listed in Appendix).

See: Ministers of Education; Education in Scotland; Secretary of State; Welsh Education.

Detention The keeping of a child or children in school after normal school hours, one of the more frequently used punishments. The time varies, but usually does not exceed a 'period' of forty minutes. Children in detention are usually set some work to do during that time. Teachers may not impose detention on a pupil on the same day as the offence is committed. At least twenty-four hours notice must be given so that parents need not worry when their children fail to arrive home at their usual time. With the gradual abolition of corporal punishment, detentions tend to be used more. However, the value of detention is open to question. To the teacher it is an extra chore he can well do without; to the pupil it represents another black mark against school as a kind of prison.

See: Discipline; Punishment.

Dip.H.E. (Diploma in Higher Education) See Diploma.

Diploma Usually below degree standard, this qualification is awarded following the successful completion of a course of study at technical and other, similar colleges. Some diplomas are awarded by universities following higher level courses in some fields. Some others are regarded as being an alternative of excellent standard to the more conventional degree, e.g.:

Diploma in Higher Education (Dip.H.E.), a comparatively new qualification, first introduced as an idea in 1972 in the White Paper *Education – A Framework for Expansion*. A report, published in June 1973 by a special working party of the Council for National Academic Awards, fully accepted the Dip.H.E. as an 'additional qualification available throughout continuing education'. There are several types of Dip.H.E., but in general, it is awarded after a successful two-year course, equivalent to two years full-time study at degree level. It is an independent qualification, which, it is hoped, will be acceptable to employers, or may be used as a credit base for further study to degree level. It is meant mainly for would-be teachers who would go on to take the B.Ed.

Diploma of Art and Design (Dip.A.D.), the equivalent of a pass degree at university, awarded at art colleges as a major qualification following an intensive course in art, usually lasting five years. It was introduced in 1961 to replace the National Diploma in Design.

See: Degree.

Direct Grant Schools Independent secondary grammar schools, generally considered to be the cream of the British education system. They receive a grant direct from the Department of Education and Science, subject to their offering at least twenty-five per cent of their places each year free of fees to pupils who have attended a state school for not less than two years before entry to the direct grant school. Up to a further twenty-five per cent of the places should be reserved for pupils whose fees will be paid by the local authorities. Half of the direct grant school places may be available for fee payers.

After a decision made by the Labour Government in 1974 to withdraw this grant from the schools from September 1976 unless they agreed to embrace the comprehensive sector, more than 100 out of the top 177 direct grant schools decided to go fully independent. The remainder, mostly Roman Catholic direct grant schools, which generally gave a far higher than average proportion of their places free of fees and could not afford to go independent, decided to become comprehensives.

The Government grant is being phased out, allowing all pupils on free places prior to September 1976 to continue at the schools without having to pay. Due to the loss of grant, those schools going independent will have to increase fees substantially.

Further reading: *Paying for Private Schools* by H. Glennerster and G. Wilson, LSE Studies on Education (Allen Lane, The Penguin Press, 1970); *The New Law of Education* by G. Taylor and J. B. Saunders (Butterworth, 1971); *Education Committees Year Book* for full list of direct grant schools, published annually (Councils and Education Press); *The Public and Preparatory Schools Year Book* and *The Girls' School Year Book* for details of top direct grant schools, published annually (A. & C. Black).

See: Comprehensive Education; Donnison Report; Public Schools.

Discipline This is the maintenance of good order in a school. It should not be equated with punishment, especially corporal punishment, often assumed necessary for discipline at school. There is the world of difference between the good teacher who has a 'well-disciplined class' and the 'disciplinarian'. Most schools have a form of prefectoral system to help teachers maintain reasonable order outside the classroom. Firm instructions by teachers inside the classroom together with lessons that arrest the pupils' attention will usually keep good discipline without resort to straps, canes, slippers, paddles or even the least effective punishment of them all – lines.

Discovery Method An educational system whereby the pupil is encouraged to find out things for himself or herself. According to the Plowden Report, finding out is preferable to being told. Unfortunately, many teachers have misinterpreted this to mean that children should be allowed to do as they please. Often, the discovery method consists merely of an out-of-school expedition on which the children are encouraged to collect and bring back to the classroom all sorts of disparate objects that they find. No attempt is made to interpret or explain the significance of the finds. For discovery methods to be successful, as indeed many are, teachers must be able to guide such discoveries carefully and combine the method of allowing the child to *believe* that he has made the discovery with the more traditional teaching methods of *telling* the child what the discovery means and how to apply it.

See: Activity Method; Plowden Report.

Discretionary Grants See Student Grants.

Divisional Executives A number of counties are divided into divisions which are allowed to administer the education within that division but which remain under the financial control and overall jurisdiction of the county authority and observe the rules and regulations laid down by the county. The divisional executive administers excepted districts of which there are about thirty, each with a population of at least 60,000 or which had more than 7000 pupils attending its elementary schools in 1939.

Don A term used for a person who teaches at a university, especially Oxford or Cambridge. It derives from the Spanish title for a nobleman and was first used in England in about 1660 to describe a senior tutor, professor or fellow.

Donnison Report The Public Schools Commission, under the chairmanship of Sir John Newsom, published the first part of this massive report in 1968 (two volumes), calling for the admission to public boarding schools of 38,000 pupils with boarding needs as an initial attempt to integrate the independent and maintained school sectors. A further three volumes were produced in 1970, when the commission was chaired by Professor David (now Lord) Donnison. This recommended the full integration of direct grant schools into the maintained sector and called for the abolition of the charitable status of other public schools. From September 1976 the phasing out of direct grant schools began. They were given the option of going fully independent, or becoming maintained comprehensive schools, or closing.

See: Direct Grant Schools; Newsom Reports; Public Schools.

Drama Association See Educational Drama Association.

Drink and Drugs The taking of hard drugs and heavy drinking among adolescents are growing problems. Although 'only' 3.6 in every 100,000 population are drug addicts and about 11 in every 1000 adults are said to have a 'serious drink problem', these figures do not present anything like a total picture of the true situation. Only about one tenth of drug takers and alcoholics are known to the authorities and no accurate figures are available from official sources.

Drug addiction in London and the conurbations is higher than elsewhere and in university towns it can be heavier still. For example, taking the national figure of 3.6 per 100,000, in Cambridge alone (with a population of 200,000) it is 23.9 per 100,000. The concern by doctors is not helped when certain factions, including even a university vice-chancellor (Prof. Lawrence Gower, vice-chancellor of Southampton University) call for the legalization of 'pot' (cannabis).

Each year brings its small harvest of suspensions and expulsions from schools (particularly public boarding schools) of boys (more so than girls) who have been *caught* smoking pot or taking other drugs (the number of users of heroin, a far 'harder' drug is showing signs of decrease).

But if drugs are a problem, drinking by schoolchildren is becoming an even greater one. Schools in the London area have over the past year detected drunkenness among pupils after the lunch break. Many are believed to frequent public houses near schools, while others have been caught with bottles of alcoholic drink.

According to research conducted by Dr S. J. Cooper, a lecturer in psychology at Belfast's Queen's University, babies could be born alcoholics or addicts if their mothers drink or take drugs during pregnancy.

Alcohol withdrawal symptoms have been noted in new-born infants when the mother had consumed alcohol during her pregnancy and a New York survey in 1963 showed that 300 babies had been born with the symptoms of addiction. These included restlessness, disturbed sleep, excessively high-pitched crying and vomiting.

Doctors are forced under the Misuse of Drugs Act, 1971, to notify to the Home Office of all drug addicts who come before them. Many, according to numerous reports, were still failing to do so. Many addicts under treatment managed to obtain illicit drugs in addition to those officially prescribed. There is a criminal black market in existence and many of the softer drugs, such as cannabis, are often sold in school playgrounds.

With alcohol, it is even more difficult to keep a tight control. Parents often leave young teenagers alone in the house to help themselves from well-stocked 'bars'.

For addresses, see Appendix.

Dual Use In 1970, the Government then in power declared that as much use as possible should be made of schools and other educational establishments. Schools in many local authorities were to be kept open in the evenings for the use of the rest of the community. For example, gymnasiums and sports complexes could be used by children and, later, by adults, who could also make use of school halls for plays, concerts and lectures: hence the term dual use or dual provision.

See: Community Schools.

Dyslexia A physiological dysfunction of the brain which shows itself in the inability to read. Like autism, dyslexia has often been wrongly diagnosed by teachers as backwardness in the child, who is often chastised for being lazy or stupid. Naturally, care has to be taken that the backward reader is not immediately dubbed as a dyslexic. Symptoms of these otherwise bright and often alert children (again, quite different from autistic children, who are withdrawn) include the inability to differentiate between such letters as 'b' and 'd' or 'p' and 'q', and the jumbling of words, sometimes reading the second syllable first or reading 'improve' as 'inrope'. Of course, beginners in reading often make these same errors and one must beware not to assume immediately that this is dyslexia. Once diagnosed, however, immediate steps should be taken to give the child remedial reading and mathematics lessons (numbers can also be confused) by experts specially trained in this complicated field. Several special schools, many of them private or voluntary, exist.

Further reading: *Developmental Dyslexia* by M. Critchley (Heinemann, 1964).

See: Autism.

E

Education Act (1944) This Act is sometimes also referred to as the Butler Act and is considered to be one of the most important pieces of educational legislation since the great Act of 1870 which introduced state education in Britain.

Mr Richard Austen Butler (now Lord Butler of Saffron Walden) was Conservative MP for Saffron Walden (1929–65) and was President of the Board of Education (1941–45). As architect of the 1944 Act, Butler abolished the Board and replaced it with a more powerful Ministry of Education (now Department of Education). The Act also abolished the rather vague concept of elementary education and introduced a tripartite scheme: primary, secondary and further, with 'secondary education for all'. It also specified the rights and duties of parents and local authorities concerning their children.

Possibly the most vital section of the Act, and certainly the one to have become the most controversial since the advent of comprehensive education, is Section 36. This states: 'It shall be the duty of the parent of every child of compulsory school age to cause him to receive efficient full-time education suitable to his age, ability and aptitude, either by regular attendance at school or otherwise.'

Parents have the duty, therefore, to ensure that their children receive 'efficient' education, though not necessarily at a school. It is the duty of the local education authority to ensure that there are sufficient suitable schools in its area to give such 'efficient' education to the children of all parents residing there.

The Act raised the statutory leaving age from fourteen to fifteen so that all children received ten full years of education from the age of five, and recommended that the leaving age be raised still further to sixteen. This proposal was shelved for nearly thirty years and had to wait until September, 1972, when Mrs Margaret Thatcher, then Secretary of State for Education and Science, implemented it.

Among other measures produced by the Butler Act were: the adoption by the state of denominational schools, either as 'voluntary aided' or 'voluntary controlled' schools; the compulsory inclusion in the curriculum of a daily assembly for worship and regular religious instruction (later known as religious education or RE); the provision of free medical and dental treatment following medical inspections in schools, free milk and free meals for children in need.

Local education authorities also became responsible for the special education of handicapped children and were free to pay fees for children at independent schools. Physical education (PE) was also made a compulsory part of the school curriculum.

The Butler Act also ensured equal pay for women teachers and saw to it that local authorities paid their teachers salaries in accordance with scales agreed by the Burnham Committee and approved by the Minister (Secretary of State).

Further Reading: *The New Law of Education* by J. G. Taylor and J. B. Saunders. (Butterworth, 1971); *Teachers and the Law* by G. R. Barrell (Methuen, 1966); *A Guide to English Schools* by T. Burgess (Penguin, 1969).

Education Acts There have been about thirty Acts of Parliament on education since the great Elementary Education Act of 1870, the most important of which was without doubt the Act of 1944, known as the Butler Act. The following is a summary of some of them.

1844 Factory Act This Act made it compulsory for parents of children who worked in the 'satanic mills' to send them to school for three full or six half days a week. It was amended in 1864 and in 1867 to do the same for children working in factories other than mills and in workshops of all kinds, respectively.

1870 Elementary Education Act William Forster (1818–86), who was vice-president of the Committee of the Privy Council for Education, was responsible for the Act which first made education compulsory for all young children. It set up school boards and allowed money for building schools to be levied from the rates. It permitted the running of non-denominational schools alongside religious schools. The former were free to decide whether or not to give religious instruction.

1876 (Lord Sandon's) Act This Act made it the parent's duty to see that his child received school instruction in reading, writing and arithmetic. It made it illegal to employ children under the age of ten. Those between ten and fourteen could only be employed if they had reached an adequate standard in the Three Rs.

1880 Elementary Education Act This Act made school boards produce by-laws on the compulsory school attendance of all children aged between five and ten.

1889 Technical Instruction Act Local authorities, the county and borough councils of the day, were allowed to levy a penny rate for technical education.

1902 Education Act This Act is sometimes referred to as the Balfour Act, because the Prime Minister had given it his full backing. It replaced the school boards with local education authorities and was the first step towards a unified education system. It allowed for secondary education and further education to be provided by the LEAs.

1906 Provision of Meals Act This Act gave local authorities power to provide meals for children at school, following findings by a Government-sponsored committee that many children were suffering from malnutrition. LEAs were given permission to levy the necessary funds from rates or from voluntary organizations.

1907 Administrative Provisions Act This Act gave LEAs power to provide medical treatment for school children, following a lengthy campaign for the setting up of health centres for this purpose by Margaret McMillan (1860–1931) who, with her sister Rachel (1859–1917), was among the great Socialist pioneers for the nursery school movement in this country. Medical inspections and treatment in schools became compulsory in 1918.

1918 Fisher Act This Act raised the school leaving age to fourteen, made it illegal to employ children under the age of twelve and allowed LEAs to open nursery schools and nursery classes for children aged between two and five. It also allowed school leavers aged fourteen to continue education at schools to be set up for the purpose. Above all, it reformed the financing of education and gave birth to what is now the rate support grant.

1936 Education Act This Act raised the school leaving age to fifteen as from 1939 (this had to be postponed owing to the outbreak of World War II on 3 September that year).

1944 Education Act See Education Act (1944).

1959 Education Act This Act raised the grants paid to voluntary aided schools from fifty per cent to seventy-five per cent so that they could provide secondary education for pupils from their own voluntary primary schools, and from twenty-five per cent to seventy-five per cent to voluntary (denominational) teacher training colleges.

1962 Education Act This Act revised arrangements for student grants and implemented the recommendations of the Crowther Report to have only two, not three, school leaving dates. These were at Easter, for those children born between September and the end of February, and July, the end of the summer term, for the remainder.

1964 Education Act This Act allowed LEAs to vary the transfer age of children from primary to secondary schools and allowed maintenance payments to those in special schools who were over statutory leaving age.

1967 Education Act This Act increased grants to aided and special agreement schools, extended the power of LEAs to defray the expenses of setting up controlled schools and provided for a system of loans in respect of capital expenditure for colleges of education.

1968 Education Act This Act clarified the law on the change of character of a school, such as the change in its size, or change from single sex to co-educational, and provided for more independent governing bodies of colleges of education and other maintained colleges.

1976 Education Act This Act made it compulsory for all LEAs to submit plans to the Secretary of State on the reorganization of their secondary schools into comprehensives, and forced them to seek the Secretary of State's permission before sending children from the authority to any fee-paying schools. In effect, this Act, bitterly opposed both by the Conservative Opposition and the House of Lords, became the major stepping-stone to universal comprehensive education in Britain.

Educational Administration Since 1903, in England and Wales, education (schools, further education/adult education colleges, colleges of education, polytechnics – but *not* universities) has been administered by the local education authorities (LEAs). Before that date, a series of local school boards were in charge of educational administration and raised the necessary revenue, as do the LEAs, from the rates. The Department of Education and Science is nationally responsible for educational policies, but LEAs are autonomous, except when forced to comply with an Education Act's law. The local councils, from which education committees are picked, are elected by the local ratepaying population on a party political basis. The education committee, aided by various subcommittees and by members co-opted because of their expertise rather than their political affiliations, takes decisions as to the type and number of schools, colleges, etc., it requires, what teachers to employ and how much money it should spend on books and equipment (on a *per capita* basis). In Scotland, local authorities and the Scottish Education Department are responsible for educational administration. Universities are autonomous but depend on central government for their finances, administered by the University Grants Committee.

See: Local Education Authority; DES; Education Committee.

Educational Advisers These are local authority advisers – there are about 2000 in the country – who form a close link between school heads and heads of departments and the local education authority. Most of them are promoted teachers whose job it is to advise schools on their curriculum and help sort out any administrative or academic problems. Some authorities also appoint special 'subject advisers', specialist teachers who give schools advice on such subjects as mathematics, science, history, special education for the educationally subnormal, immigrant education, as well as curriculum development and in-service training. The terms educational adviser and local authority inspector are often used synonymously. They are used in every field of education, including primary, secondary, special, further and higher education.

Educational Drama Association Voluntary association of teachers and lecturers in drama, founded in 1943 to help teachers run courses in schools, ranging from nurseries to colleges. It runs a children's theatre company, a dance group and an annual summer school attended by members from Britain and abroad.

For address to contact, see Appendix.

Educational Institute of Scotland See Education in Scotland.

Educationally Subnormal (ESN) Description given to children who, 'by reason of limited ability or other conditions resulting in educational retardation, require some specialized form of education wholly or partly in substitution for education normally given in ordinary schools', (*The Handicapped Pupils and Special School Regulations*, pamphlet no. 365, Ministry of Education, HMSO, 1959). At present, there are more than 1300 special schools catering for about 113,000 children deemed to be ESN. Admission to such schools usually follows the recommendations of teachers to the local authority and children are first examined by the area's medical officer, in case special defects come to light (deafness, poor sight or partial blindness). Schools are both of the day and residential variety. Some children, considered to be ESN, remain in ordinary schools and are given special lessons in remedial classes. They are more often referred to as 'slow learners'. An ESN child is one whose IQ is generally in the range from fifty to seventy, although children with IQs of up to about eighty-five may also be admitted to special schools if this is considered necessary.

Further reading: *Special Education in England and Wales* (Oxford University Press, 1969).

See: Remedial Classes; Slow Learners.

Educational Priority Area (EPA) It was the Plowden Report which proposed that areas with poor, inadequate housing, old, dilapidated schools and a high incidence of social deprivation, should be termed 'educational priority areas'. Such areas, it recommended, should become the subject of 'positive discrimination' and receive higher grants from Government funds for schools than areas where children were socially better off.

See: Plowden Report,; Positive Discrimination.

Educational Psychology A movement dating back probably to Plato, gaining momentum with Rousseau's *Emile*, but taking root with the *Biographical Sketch of an Infant* by Charles Darwin in 1877. Unlike Plato's more philosophical approach, Darwin's work studied the gradual development of a child as well as its behavioural patterns. In 1896 a psychological laboratory was opened at University College, London, by James Sully, the college's Professor of Logic. Teachers could bring their more difficult pupils to the laboratory for examination and treatment. Sully became inaugural president of the British Child Study Association set up two years before the opening of his laboratory. Gradually, Sully's methods of sympathetic understanding for children's problems and difficulties and his diagnostic brilliance attracted teachers and school inspectors. But it was not until early this century that educational psychology became officially recognized with the appointment of Cyril Burt by the London County Council as the first-ever local authority educational psychologist. It gave rise to the use in selection of IQ tests. The work of Jean Piaget, Schonell, Bernstein, Jencks, among many others, brought the psychology of education into full bloom. It also gave rise to many of the progressive reforms in education and to some of its present problems.

Further reading: *A Short History of British Psychology* by L. S. Hearnshaw (Methuen, 1964): *Educational Objectives and the Teaching of Educational Psychology* by E. Stones and D. Anderson (Methuen, 1972).

See: Burt, Sir Cyril; Froebel, Friedrich; Montessori Method; Piaget, Jean; Schonell, Sir Fred.

Education Committee A group of people drawn from the elected town, city or county councillors to run the local authority's education, including the maintained schools, further education colleges and polytechnics which are in its area. It usually reflects the same political majority as the main council and has various subcommittees responsible for different aspects of educational administration and finance; a Schools Subcommittee, responsible for maintained schools and teachers, a Finance and General Purposes Committee, etc.

See: Local Education Authorities.

Education Correspondents Group A body first convened in 1961 at the suggestion of Charles Birdsall, then Press Officer of the Ministry of Education, by Roy Nash, who was at that time education writer of the *News Chronicle*. Membership is open to full-time education correspondents of national daily and Sunday newspapers, radio, television, the Press Association and the educational Press, as well as full-time educational freelance writers at the discretion of the committee. Its main purposes are to ease the flow of information on educational matters, to organize visits for members to overseas educational establishments and to improve educational standards and the understanding of educational problems by the general public. Lists of members (there are about fifty) are available to interested organizations on request from the Secretary.

For address to contact, see Appendix.

Education Cuts The 'cuts' became almost a household word in the mid-seventies. Public expenditure had to be severely decreased as the value of the pound dropped dramatically and the cost of living increased. It was found that Britain was spending too much on its services. Education was made to take the brunt of the cuts. As most of public expenditure (about seventy per cent) in education went on teacher salaries, cut-backs had to be made in other sectors of this big field: school buildings, school meals, audio-visual equipment, classroom materials, non-teaching staff, school transport, textbooks, swimming lessons, school visits, and, biggest of all, the employment of teachers.

Education in Scotland Education in Scotland is in many vital respects different from that in England and Wales. In some entries of this reference book, these differences have been outlined. The following section summarizes the most important of them.

Scottish Education Department (SED) The London-based Department of Education and Science (DES), has no jurisdiction over education in Scotland, other than its universities. All other educational matters fall under the SED and the Secretary of State for Scotland who has a Parliamentary under-Secretary with specific responsibilities for education.

Local Education Authorities (LEA) In Scotland, the responsibility for educational administration used to rest with thirty-one county councils and four city councils. These ceased to exist after May 1975 when local government in Scotland was reorganized. They were replaced by nine regional councils, a number of district councils and three island councils. Educational administration rests solely with the regional and island councils.

Terms within Local Government England: borough; Scotland: burgh; England: Mayor/Lord Mayor; Scotland: Provost/Lord Provost; England: Treasurer; Scotland: Chamberlain (burghs), Treasurer (county); England: Alderman (elected by the council, not the electorate); Scotland: Bailie – this has no equivalent in English terms and is not strictly speaking the equivalent of Alderman. The bailie is a magistrate of a burgh court, elected from other elected councillors.

Grant-aided Schools More or less like the direct grant schools of England and Wales, they are run by voluntary managers and are in receipt of a direct Government grant.

Public Schools All independent schools in Scotland have to be registered provisionally until their standards have been inspected and passed as reasonable by the inspectorate. South of the Border, independent schools 'recognized as efficient' need not be registered officially.

Primary Schools Courses in Scottish primary schools last from the age of five to twelve, whereas in England and Wales, they last from the age of five to eleven. However, the middle school system is similar to the Scottish seven-year primary course.

Curriculum Whereas this is the responsibility in England of the Schools Council, it is the Consultative Committee on the Curriculum set up by the Secretary of State for Scotland in 1965, which advises on Scotland's school curriculum and keeps it under constant review. Unlike the Schools Council, it has no responsibilities for examinations at national level.

Examinations The Scottish Certificate of Education is awarded to successful candidates by the Scottish Certificate of Education Examining Board. This board was set up as an independent statutory body to conduct this single leaving examination, whereas in England, examinations are recommended by the Schools Council and awarded by nine examining bodies for the General Certificate of Education (GCE) and thirteen bodies for the Certificate of Secondary Education (CSE). In England the GCE consists of two levels: Ordinary (O-level) taken normally after five years of secondary education, and Advanced (A-level) taken after seven years. In Scotland, there are three levels:

Ordinary Grade (*O-Grade*) which is more or less equivalent to the O-level of GCE, is taken after four years of secondary education (since secondary education starts at twelve-plus, the age is about the same as for O-level);

Higher Grade (*H-Grade*) which is taken in the fifth or sixth year of secondary education. Highers are not quite the same as the English A-level, since Scottish pupils are expected to take up to five Higher subjects within a fairly broad curriculum (instead of one, two or three A-levels at GCE);

Certificate of Sixth Year Studies which is more like the A-level, since it represents an in-depth study of two or three subjects.

Unlike English grammar schools and many English comprehensive schools, Scottish schools do not have a split sixth form (arts and sciences) but follow a broader curriculum and, in general, manage to pass more (indeed, proportionally significantly more) candidates to universities.

School Management State-maintained schools in Scotland are not required to have boards of management or government as in England.

Higher Education While universities still fall under the aegis of the Department of Education and Science in London, other institutions of higher education, such as colleges of education, are controlled financially by the Scottish Education Department and administratively by boards of governors.

Universities Scotland has some of the finest universities in the United Kingdom, of which the oldest (St Andrews, Glasgow, Aberdeen and Edinburgh) offer four-year courses (unlike England's three-year courses) for first degrees: M.A. (Master of Arts, unlike English universities' B.A. first) and B.Sc. The Scottish 'Ordinary' degree, which covers a wide range of disciplines, is rapidly gaining popularity in English and Welsh universities. It was highly commended in the Robbins Report. Scotland's new universities have also rapidly distinguished themselves. Stirling, on a beautiful campus, was started from scratch; Strathclyde was formerly the Glasgow Royal College of Science and Technology; Dundee was originally incorporated with St Andrews; and Heriot-Watt, now with its own Charter, was affiliated to the University of Edinburgh in 1933.

St Andrews, Glasgow and Aberdeen were all founded in the fifteenth century as episcopal foundations, while Edinburgh was set up as a civic university in 1583.

Teachers Scotland has about 56,000 teachers, whose salaries are the responsibility of the Scottish Teachers' Salaries Committee, set up by the Secretary of State for Scotland (they do not come under the Burnham Committees, unlike teachers in England and Wales).

Only those teachers who are registered with the General Teaching Council for Scotland (there is no equivalent body in England and Wales) may be appointed to permanent teaching posts in public (i.e. state-maintained) and grant-aided schools. The council was constituted in 1966 after recommendations contained in the 1963 Report of the Committee on the Teaching Profession of Scotland (chaired by Lord Wheatley).

It keeps standards of education, training and the 'fitness to teach' of all would-be entrants to the teaching profession under constant review, recommends the number of teachers that is required and keeps an up-to-date register of all teachers who are fully qualified. Like the General Medical Council in England, the GTC (Scotland) investigates all matters of discipline regarding teachers and is empowered to remove from its register any teacher guilty of professional misconduct or those convicted of any criminal or other offences. Decisions to delete names from the register are subject to appeal to the Court of Session. The council has forty-five members, thirty of them certificated teachers. The latter come from primary and secondary schools, further education centres and colleges of education. Other appointed members represent the Association of County Councils in Scotland, the Scottish Counties and Cities Association, Association of Directors of Education in Scotland, the Scottish universities and the Churches. The Council is elected every four years.

Social Services Whereas in England and Wales, the responsibility for social work services is discharged through the Department of Health and Social Security, in Scotland it is the responsibility of the Education Department's own Social Work Services Group, with the exception of financial schemes such as National Insurance and Supplementary Benefits. These fall under the Secretary of State for Social Services in Scotland.

Approved Schools (Community Homes) In England and Wales there are 120 approved schools (now known as community homes) whose responsibility is discharged by the local authorities. In Scotland these schools are known as List D Schools. There are twenty-seven, two of them run by a local authority (Glasgow) and the remainder by voluntary authorities and central Government.

Educational Institute of Scotland The biggest of the Scottish teachers' unions, representing more than 30,000 members. It serves to promote higher standards of teaching and to improve conditions for Scotland's teachers.

The Institute was founded in 1847 and granted a Royal Charter in 1851. It has played a leading role in negotiating the salaries for Scottish teachers and in procuring a properly set out contract for all teachers, including the number of hours that should be spent in the classroom and on many other activities, such as marking and preparation of lessons. Negotiations for the contract were finalized in 1976. Teachers south of the border do not enjoy such a contract.

For addresses see Appendix.

Further reading: *Public Education in Scotland* (Scottish Education Department, 1972); *Scottish Educational Statistics* (published annually by HMSO); *The Scottish Educational System* by F. L. Hunter (Pergamon Press).

Education Officer See Chief Education Officer.

Education Shop An original idea to give parents an advice and information service from an ordinary 'shop' in the High Street. The first one was set up at Ipswich in 1965 by the Advisory Centre for Education (ACE). The aim was to give working-class parents the chance to inquire into educational problems while doing their shopping. Whereas ACE received and answered some 5000 letters a year from articulate, middle-class parents, very few were received from poorer parents. The idea has spread to other cities.

See: Advisory Centre for Education.

Education Welfare Officer Once known more ominously as the 'truancy officer', the education welfare officer is employed by the local education authority to deal with school attendance problems and the general welfare of school children. His or her work takes the officer into the children's homes as well as schools.

For address to contact, see Appendix.

Eleven-plus An examination taken towards the end of a child's primary school education and used as a selection method for secondary schools. Pupils who pass the examination are normally selected for grammar schools; those who fail enter secondary modern schools. With the reorganization of secondary education and the increasing development of comprehensive schools, the eleven-plus is gradually disappearing and comparatively few local education authorities still retain these tests. Some still use it to select children for direct grant schools, but these, too, are to be phased out and many have already decided to go fully independent or join the state sector. It used to be known as the Scholarship Examination.

At a rough estimate, eighty per cent of those who entered the eleven-plus went to secondary modern schools while twenty per cent went to grammar schools. In each case, there was a margin of error to about ten per cent. In other words, one tenth of those in secondary moderns should have been selected for grammar schools, while one tenth of grammar pupils should have been sent to the secondary moderns. Some of those who failed the eleven-plus were later (often at about the age of thirteen) transferred to grammar schools through the wisdom of their teachers.

See: Comprehensive Education; Direct Grant Schools.

Employment of Children By law, the minimum age at which a child may be employed is two years less than the maximum school leaving age. At present, the leaving age being sixteen, a child will have to be fourteen to be employed – but then only for a maximum of two hours a day and never during school hours. Employment of such a child may not start before 7 a.m. or last later than 7 p.m. and it may not be in such a field of work as to prejudice the child's health or educational opportunities. Despite these and other clearly laid-down conditions, the law is regularly abused with children being made to work long hours in hotels, pubs and clubs, super-markets and theatres. The law is based on the Children and Young Persons Act of 1933 (amended 1963 and 1965) and also in regulations provided in Section 59 of the Education Act (1944).

Further reading: *The New Law of Education* by G. Taylor and J. B. Saunders (Butterworth, 1971).

Employment of School Leavers During the summer months unemployment figures tend to swing upwards, augmented by the number of jobless school leavers. In 1976, out of about 750,000 leavers, some 450,000 failed to find a job within a month or two of leaving school. Jobless leavers may sign on as unemployed. They may seek employment through the normal channels (advertisements, recommendations, etc.) or through agencies set up by the special Youth Employment section of the Department and the local authority. Careers officers of local authorities or school careers teachers (where these are appointed) often assist school leavers to find jobs while they are in their last stages of schooling.

For address to contact, see Appendix.

Employment of Teachers Teachers can be employed either on a permanent or a temporary basis to teach at a particular school or be sent to any one of many schools within a local education authority. The LEA is the employer and pays the salary of the teacher. The authority is usually represented at an initial interview that the teacher seeking employment will have with the head teacher of the school which has advertised the post. A manager or governor is also likely to be present. Where the authority has advertised for a supply teacher (one who can be sent to any school within the autho-rity's jurisdiction), the interview is conducted between the candidate and LEA representatives. Part-time teachers are paid at a ratio of full-time appointed teachers' salaries.

See: Burnham Committees.

Environmentalist One who believes that the environment shapes our intelligence and that the development of intelligence depends greatly on how we are brought up, in what kind of home, what kind of street, rather than on what we inherit from our father and mother and other ancestors. The environmentalist, to put it in crudely oversimplified terms, believes that eighty per cent of our intelligence comes from the environment and only twenty per cent is inherited. Those favouring the influence of genetics in the development of intelligence see things the other way about. These differences are often called the 'nature versus nurture' controversy.

See: Burt, Sir Cyril; Genetics; Intelligence Quotient (IQ).

Environmental Studies A combination of geography, history, social studies, biology and economics used to study the environment, thus allowing the child greater opportunity to look at his own surroundings and learn from them. Sociological surveys among the local population, interviews of elderly citizens by the pupils to see how things have changed since their time, visits to cemetries with inspections of old gravestones, church records, etc., help the child to understand not only his environment but to grasp the basic principles of sociology, history and other subjects.

Further reading: *Environmental Studies* by G. Martin and E. R. A. Turner (Blond, 1972).

EPA See Educational Priority Area.

Equal Opportunity or **Equality of Opportunity** The policy adopted by the Labour Party in the 1950s to scrap the eleven-plus selection test which divided able and less able children into grammar and secondary modern schools and to provide for the opportunity of all-ability groups to be educated together in one kind of school (comprehensive). In 1964, with a Labour Government, the reorganization of secondary schools started. Equal opportunity has often been misinterpreted to mean that all children are equal, instead of meaning that all should be given the same chance in education.

Further reading: *All Our Future* by J. W. B. Douglas and others (Peter Davis, 1968); *Inside Comprehensive Schools* by T. Burgess (HMSO, 1970); *Social Class and the Comprehensive School* by J. Ford (Routledge and Kegan Paul, 1969).

See: Comprehensive Education; Eleven-plus.

ESN See Educationally Subnormal.

Evening Classes At least 1,750,000 people aged from sixteen to ninety-plus attend evening courses at institutes of education throughout the country, to study subjects from accountancy to Zen. For a comparatively small fee, within the reach of most people's pockets (fees may be waived for the very needy and senior citizens at the discretion of the local authority), these institutes cater for a wide range of tastes in knowledge, although in recent years the cuts in public expenditure have forced some authorities to close a number of courses, particularly those of a non-vocational nature. Classes are normally held in schools or technical colleges. Most of the lecturers are employed on a part-time basis and the institutes are run by local education authorities. Usually, though not always, at least fifteen students are required to enrol before a course can commence.

Examinations Schools provide a number of written, practical and oral examinations as well as teachers' assessments of pupils based on their work over the term, year or years. There are also internal examinations to assure pupil progress. The main examinations, in the past, present and future are:

Eleven-plus See separate article under Eleven-plus.

School Certificate (SC) See separate articles under School Certificate and Higher School Certificate.

General Certificate of Education (GCE) This examination, also taken in two parts, replaced the School Certificate and Higher School Certificate in 1951 and is still taken throughout the country (except in Scotland, which is treated separately in this book). The major difference between the SC and HSC and the GCE is that, whereas the passing of the former depended on groups of subjects being passed, the GCE is awarded in each of the subjects that the candidate has passed. The GCE is set, marked and administered by eight examining boards.

The first part, **Ordinary Level (O-level),** is usually taken at the age of sixteen (sometimes earlier in special circumstances, or later) and can be in any number of subjects that the candidate and his/her teachers think suitable. The number normally ranges between four and nine subjects.

The second part, **Advanced Level (A-level),** is usually taken at the age of eighteen. Again, any number of subjects is possible, but generally two or three are attempted. Standards are high and three A-levels at good grades (A-level at grade A is the highest possible, grade E is the lowest) would normally ensure a university place, though many universities accept a series of lower grades.

One important aspect of the GCE is that both O-levels and A-levels can be 'collected', one at a time if need be, to make up the requisite number of qualifications demanded by employers, colleges or universities.

Certificate of Secondary Education (CSE) From 1951 to 1965, the GCE was the most important examination for school leavers. But it was found that too many pupils were leaving schools without any form of qualification, particularly those pupils at secondary modern schools. Many teachers clamoured for an examination which they could administer themselves, and the CSE met most of the demands. Subject-based, it is usually taken at the age of sixteen and is of a generally lower standard than GCE O-level. Although it is run by fourteen regional examining bodies, all have a majority of teachers from the schools participating in the examinations.

It is graded from 1–5 or 'ungraded' (i.e. fail). A grade 1 is equivalent to a pass at O-level. Any number of subjects may be taken and certificates are awarded even if only one CSE subject is passed. The examination syllabus is often chosen by the teachers themselves and marked by them, but is moderated by external examiners (see Modes 1–3).

Certificate of Education (Foundation) This examination is, at the time of writing, creating heated controversy and is expected to replace both GCE O-levels and the CSE by 1980–1. Proposed by working parties of the Schools Council, it will present a single examination system, virtually controlled by teachers themselves, for all pupils aged sixteen-plus. It, too, is to be graded (from 1–7) but, according to proposals, the first grade is to be subdivided into 1A, 1B and 1C, equivalent to the first three grades of the present O-level. See separate article on Certificate of Education.

Certificate of Extended Education (CEE) This is another newcomer to the examination field. It is aimed at what is known as the New Sixth – those children aged sixteen and seventeen who, before the raising of the school leaving age, would have left school at fifteen but who would like to try some kind of examination after spending a year in the sixth form. Papers will be pitched at a relatively low level for pupils not bright enough to sit for the GCE A-level. Candidates will be awarded one of four grades if they enter the examination, which will have no 'fail' classification.

Common Entrance Examination In 1903 it was decided that a common examination should be set for candidates wishing to enter public schools and the first such examination was set in 1904. At that stage, the joint-committee set up to develop and write the examination consisted of four members of the Headmasters' Conference and three of the Incorporated Association of Preparatory Schools, but only twenty-five public schools were willing to join the scheme. Today, most HMC and IAPS schools operate such a system, with examinations being held on various dates in February,

June and November. Papers are in English, mathematics and French as well as history, geography and a number of optional papers. There is an entrance fee. For addresses to contact, see Appendix.

Further reading: *Examinations and English Education* by S. Wiseman (Manchester University Press, 1961); *Examinations – An Account of their Evolution as Administrative Devices in England* by J. Montgomery (Longmans, 1965); *The Reliability of GCE O-level Examinations in English Language* (Joint Matriculation Board, 1967); *The 1968 CSE Monitoring Experiment*, Schools Council Working Paper 34 (Evans-Methuen Educational, 1971); *A Guide to English Schools* by T. Burgess (Penguin, 1969); *The Public and Preparatory Schools Year Book* and *The Girls' School Year Book*, both published annually (A. & C. Black).

See: A-level; Examining Boards; Headmasters' Conference (HMC); Incorporated Association of Preparatory Schools (IAPS); O-level; ONC; OND.

Examining Boards At present, there are eight separate boards that set examinations and syllabi for the Ordinary ('O') and Advanced ('A') levels in the General Certificate of Education (GCE) and fourteen boards setting examinations for the Certificate of Secondary Education (CSE). Each of the boards designs its own syllabus, and, in most cases (See Modes) sets the examination questions, marks the answers and publishes the results. Universities set up the first boards well over a century ago and are still closely connected in the running of six out of the eight GCE boards. The boards award the all-important grades to pupils sitting the examinations (A-levels are divided up into Grades A, B, C, D, E and an O, which means that the candidate has not managed to gain an A-level but was good enough to pass the examination at GCE O-level). Universities demand certain grades at A-level for entry, which can vary, according to subject, from two A-levels at Grade D to three A-levels at Grade A (the latter is often demanded by Oxford and Cambridge). Polytechnics generally tend to accept lower grades than universities for admission.

Standards tend to vary from board to board and it is difficult to recommend boards for their 'easy' or 'difficult' examinations. The percentage of pupils within each grade rarely differs beyond a few percentage points, since most numbers have been laid down by the Schools Council. In other words, the same, or roughly the same number of pupils will pass each year at Grade A, Grade B and so on in the major subjects.

Many schools – and certainly many parents – are often surprised by results. Some pupils who were expected by their teachers to do extremely well in examinations, fail or are awarded grades well below expectations. For an additional fee, schools (not parents) may query results and have papers re-marked. If mistakes in original marking are noted and the candidate is re-graded as a result, the fee is generally refunded.

Most of the GCE boards set O and A-level examinations in the summer with a chance for a re-sit at O-level in the autumn (the London University Board and the Associated Examining Board also have A-level re-sits in January).

For addresses to contact, see Appendix.

Excepted District See Divisional Executives.

Expulsion Only an independent school may expel pupils and it does so if the head considers that a very serious offence has been committed by a pupil or group of pupils. Such offences could include drug-taking or the peddling of dangerous drugs (heroin, LSD) within the school, drunkenness, violence, vandalism, etc. Some such schools might expel a pupil for blatant breach of school rules, such as going to a part of the town deemed 'out of bounds' or smoking.

Where state-maintained schools are concerned, a pupil can be expelled only if he/she has passed the statutory school leaving age of sixteen. Otherwise, the pupil may only be suspended for a limited period.

See: Punishment; Suspension.

Extended Day A recommendation made by the Newsom Report of 1963 that the normal two-session school day, which stretches from about 9 a.m. until 4 p.m., should be extended for pupils in their last two years at school, so that they may take part in extra-curricular activities, such activities to be 'recognized as an integral part of the total educational programme'.

See: Newsom Reports.

External Degrees Apart from the Open University degree courses, the only degrees which may be taken externally are those of the University of London. Tuition is offered by a number of correspondence colleges. For information on entry requirements, syllabuses and courses, see address in Appendix.

F

Fagging Term given to the act of performing menial tasks by younger pupils for prefects at public schools. Fags are (or rather, were, since the practice is rapidly dying out) small boys, usually first formers, who would run errands for prefects, clean their shoes and the like and make their tea. The origin of the word is not clear.

See: Prefects.

Family Grouping or **Vertical Grouping** Instead of placing children in classes according to their age and ability, some schools – mostly infant schools – group them across several ages, generally ranging from five to seven. Thus, the same class might have brothers and sisters or cousins aged five, six and seven together. A number of such schools have found that younger children tend to learn to read more quickly in the presence of older, more expreienced readers.

Federal University A university which has a number of autonomous colleges that arrange their own courses and award their own degrees. Two such universities exist in Britain: London, which is the biggest with more than 30,000 students, and Wales. The latter has five colleges: Cardiff, Bangor, Aberystwyth, Lampeter and Swansea, as well as the Welsh National School of Medicine and the University of Wales Institute of Science and Technology (UWIST), both at Cardiff. London has three major colleges (King's, Queen Mary, University College) and three specialist colleges (Imperial and Chelsea Colleges of Science and Technology, and the London School of Economics, which is a limited company). In both cases (Wales and London) the colleges are united as one federation under the university's charter.

See: Universities.

Fees All parents pay school fees of one kind or another. Although state-maintained schools are not 'fee-paying' schools in the strict sense, the cost of the education at those schools, nevertheless, comes out of rates and taxes. It could be argued that parents whose children attend independent schools pay fees twice – once for their own children's education and again, out of taxes, for other people's children attending maintained schools. Public school fees, whether day or boarding, have risen rapidly in the past few years, so rapidly that any figure given here is likely to be out of date. Suffice it to say that day school fees are likely to range from £650 to £1000 a year, while boarding fees can average anything from £1300 to £2000. Some independent schools give scholarships and exhibitions; some give free places to deserving scholars. Parents with children at state boarding schools may have to contribute towards costs. Some local authorities send bright children from less well off homes to independent schools and meet the fees out of rates, but this is becoming increasingly rare as a result of Labour Government pressure.

A number of insurance companies offer schemes for parents and grandparents, whereby fees work out 'less expensive'. Obviously, the earlier such a scheme is entered, the cheaper it becomes and parents with serious intentions of sending sons or daughters to public schools should consult such organizations shortly after the child is born!

Further reading: *The Public and Preparatory Schools Year Book* and *The Girls' School Year Book* are published annually by A. & C. Black, with full descriptions of most good public schools, together with fees (the latter should always be double-checked); *Scholarships at Boys' Public Schools* and *Scholarships at Girls' Schools*, both published by Truman and Knightley Educational Trust.

See: Public Schools.

FEVER (Friends of the Education Voucher Experiment in Representative Regions) An organization supporting the voucher system in Britain, it is a pressure group that has had a certain amount of influence in persuading some local education authorities, such as Kent, to conduct feasibility studies into the scheme. A number of MPs (Keith Speed, Richard Wainwright, Dr Rhodes Boyson) and academics (Professors Alan Peacock, Jack Wiseman, Charles Rowley) figure among its patrons.

For address to contact, see Appendix.

See: Voucher System.

Financial Aid Parents drawing supplementary benefits because their income is too low to meet various normal expenses are able to obtain financial assistance for a number of educational charges. Although state education is free and no tuition, books or equipment need to be paid for separately by parents (the payment comes out of income tax and rates), items such as school meals, uniforms (where these are compulsory), clothing for physical education, sports and swimming, fares and school trips have to be paid for by parents. Special assistance is given to parents for the following:

School Meals Children whose parents draw supplementary benefits or whose income falls below a certain subsistence level may receive free meals at school. This level is reviewed annually by the Government of the day. For details, parents should enquire at their local Department of Employment or Social Security Office.

Uniforms Grants are given in the form of a voucher to parents earning below the recognized subsistence level, which they may trade in at a named shop for the required uniform. These amounts are also reviewed at intervals. At present, grants stand at £20 and are made at eleven-plus, when the child enters secondary school, as well as at thirteen-plus and fifteen.

Clothing Allowance Amounts are the same as for uniforms and are given to parents whose children are served free school meals. The grants are to provide the child with essential clothing, including shoes, coats, plimsolls and shorts for physical education and swimming trunks/sports' shorts. Grants are determined by way of a means test.

Fares Children on free meals are also eligible for a free travel voucher for journeys by public transport to and from school. Other children, not eligible for free meals, also travel free of charge on buses if the shortest walking distance between home and school is more than two miles (for children up to the age of eight) or three miles (for children over the age of eight). At the time of writing, the question of free fares is understood to be under review and might, in time, be abolished.

School Trips Financial assistance may be obtained from most local authorities if parents are in need. There is no hard and fast rule here and each case has to be reviewed on merit but generally local authorities are sympathetic and are opposed to leaving any child behind while the rest of his/her class or year goes on a school journey or excursion, merely because the child's parents cannot afford to pay.

Maintenance Grants These are given to parents of children staying at school beyond the statutory leaving age of sixteen. They depend on parental earnings and the size of the family and vary from as little as £12 to about £170.

School head teachers and local offices of the Department of Education, the Department of Employment, Social Security, Social Services, the Local Education Authority information offices and the Citizens Advice Bureau would be able to give parents more detailed and up-to-date information on all the above. Interviews on matters such as this should be kept confidential, and usually are, if parents ask in advance to see officials concerned privately.

See: Grants; School Meals; Uniform.

First School A school catering for the first stage of a child's education, from the age of five to the age of eight, nine or ten. It is usually the first stage of a three-tier system of schooling. Pupils would generally move on to a middle school.

See: Middle School.

Form Entry The number of pupils in each form of a school. This decides the size of the entire school. Normally, one reckons that a form, or class, will contain thirty to forty pupils. If each year group is divided into four forms, each with, say thirty-five pupils, the school takes in 140 pupils a year and is known as a 'four form entry school'. Such a school would have about 840 children in all. Some comprehensive schools are ten form entry schools: thus, they have an intake of 350 children and a total of about 2000 pupils, including the sixth form.

Free Activity Period A period during the school day, and listed as such on the timetable, when children in the class are encouraged to choose for themselves what subject they would like to tackle.

Free Period This has two possible meetings. The more common is when a class is free to undertake private study without the supervision of a teacher. The other is when a teacher has not been allocated to a class.

Free Schools These are small, progressive schools, many of them in old converted houses, that cater for children who, for one reason or another, do not attend conventional schools. Such children include school phobics, habitual truants or those whose parents prefer the type of education offered at a free school. Generally, they are run along informal lines by voluntary organizations, private individuals or social workers, and feature discussions between teachers and pupils. They try to rekindle an interest in education and learning. Most depend on grants from local authorities.

Froebel, Friedrich (1782–1852) German educational philosopher and father of the kindergarten movement. Two of his disciples opened the first kindergarten in Britain in 1851. Children, according to his views, should be encouraged rather than repressed from an early age. He believed strongly in allowing the child to discover through play, but was misinterpreted later by teachers who believed that 'discovery through play' need not be structured and closely guided. In 1938, the National Froebel Foundation was set up in London, more than sixty years after the formation of a Froebel Society in Britain.

For address to contact, see Appendix.

See: Educational Psychology; Kindergarten.

Functional Literacy The minimum level of literacy skill required to live and participate in society. What this level is, is arguable. W. S. Gray's survey for UNESCO in 1956 said that Americans, to be functionally literate, should be able to attain the standard reached by pupils in Grade Four of schooling (i.e. those aged ten). More recently, it has been suggested that adults are exposed to all kinds of reading material of greater complexity and that the level should be raised to Grade Nine (age fifteen). It could be argued that very few fifteen-year-olds are able to tackle an income tax return form or really understand a national insurance guide. It has been estimated that Britain has about two million functional illiterates (some estimates go as high as three million but there is no absolute proof for either figure). Certainly, there are at least a million adults with a reading age below nine who cannot read simple recipes or even the Highway Code.

Further reading: *The Teaching of Reading and Writing* by W. S. Gray (UNESCO, 1956); *Readability of Newspapers* by D. Moyle and others (Edge Hill College of Education, 1973); *A Language for Life* – the Bullock Report (HMSO, 1975).

See: Illiteracy.

Further Education (FE) Full-time or part-time education for people who have completed their secondary schooling. The term does not embrace courses in teacher training at colleges of education or advanced (degree) courses at polytechnics or universities. These come under higher education. FE normally describes non-advanced courses (i.e. below degree standard) at colleges of technology, further education institutes, colleges of commerce, schools and colleges of art, or at evening institutes.

Further reading: *British Further Education* by A. J. Peters (Pergamon Press, 1967); *A Plan for Polytechnics and Other Colleges* (Department of Education and Science, Cmnd 3006, HMSO 1966); *Technical Education in Britain* (Central Office of Information 1962); *Directory of Further Education* (Hobsons Press, for CRAC; see CRAC).

Further Education Information Service (FEIS) The FEIS

operates in August and September to help school leavers obtain a place on a suitable course of higher education. Each local education authority's Local Advisory Officer receives weekly vacancy lists from the DES showing the current unfilled places on degree and HND courses in polytechnics and other colleges of further education. The careers officer or local education authority can help school leavers to contact their Local Advisory Officer.

G

General Certificate of Education (GCE) See Examinations.
Genetics The branch of biology that deals with those characteristics of an offspring that are transmitted by its parents (heredity). While some human characteristics, such as the colour of eyes, are known to be determined genetically, there has been much controversy over the degree to which intelligence is inherited. Some argue that intelligence is largely inherited but others hold that it is determined by the influence of the environment.

See: Burt, Sir Cyril; Environmentalist.
Gifted Child Although educationists have been quick to recognize the need to help the mentally or physically handicapped child, the work in the area of mentally gifted children has been comparatively sparse. There are thousands of children whose true abilities have remained unrecognized by most state-maintained schools, so much so that many such children have turned into drop-outs or gang leaders and disrupters. It is often difficult to identify the gifted child without measuring IQ (mostly 140-plus). Symptoms, if that is the right word, vary. The child may appear remote, lazy, cheeky, a social renegade, often unwilling to read or write or follow the work set by the teacher. Yet when confronted with abstract problems the gifted child will be able to discuss it and solve it with comparative ease. Some gifted children lean towards the creative arts, others to mathematics and the sciences. It takes a gifted teacher to meet the challenge and recognize the child that is ready for complex O or even A-level work at the age of twelve.

The foundation of the National Association for Gifted Children has done much to highlight the problem and encourage further research in this area. It has sponsored international conferences which have shown gifted children to be of world-wide concern.

For address to contact, see Appendix.

Further reading: *Gifted Children* by M. Branch and A. Cash (Souvenir Press, 1966); *Educating Gifted Children* by D. G. Haan and H. Havighurst (Chicago University Press); *Introduction to the Gifted* by E. Hildreth (McGraw-Hill, 1966); *Teaching Clever Children, 7–11* by N. R. Tempest (Routledge & Kegan Paul, 1974); *The Children on the Hill* by M. Deakin (André Deutsch, 1972).

See: Backwardness.

Girls' Public Day School Trust (GPDST) An exclusive small body founded in 1872 with a membership of twenty-three schools. Of these, twenty-two are direct grant schools which are administered by the Trust.

For address to contact, see Appendix.

Girls' Schools Association (GSA) This is a comparatively new association, founded in December 1973, and is the nearest equivalent among girls' schools to the HMC (Headmasters' Conference). It covers more types of school than the HMC and is open to the heads of independent, direct grant and boarding schools, all in the independent sector. It was formed out of the former Association of Independent and Direct Grant Schools, which was a subsection of the Association of Headmistresses.

See: Headmasters' Conference.

Gordonstoun This public school (mixed) at Elgin, in the beautiful Moray area of Scotland, was founded in 1934 by Dr Kurt Hahn. A brilliant scholar, his great ambition was to educate children in accordance with the philosophy of Plato – that the Good must be properly trained to rule the Republic and must be taught literature, music, mathematics and rigorous physical education. Gordonstoun, starting with a handful of pupils, followed the same pattern as Hahn's original school, Salem, in Germany. Hahn, who openly opposed the Hitler regime, was thrown into a concentration camp but was eventually brought penniless to Britain. Gordonstoun soon became as famous as the still flourishing Salem. Prince Philip was among its pupils, as was Prince Charles and Prince Edward. Hahn gave Prince Philip the idea for the Duke of Edinburgh Award Scheme.

Further reading: *Gordonstoun* by F. R. G. Chew (University of Aberdeen Press, 1963).

Governors and Managers, Board of According to the instruments of government and of management, local education authorities must appoint boards of managers (for primary schools) and governors (for secondaries, colleges of further education, polytechnics and other institutions of further and higher education), while the Secretary of State for Education and Science must order such appointments for voluntary schools. At the latter, between one third and two thirds of the managers/governors are appointed by the voluntary foundation, depending on whether they are voluntary aided, controlled or special arrangement schools.

Generally, these bodies deal with the day-to-day management of the school. They appoint the head teacher and play a role in the appointment of assistant teachers following consultations with the head. Suspensions and expulsions of pupils have to be approved by them and they investigate complaints or proposals made by parents if these have been referred to them in the first instance.

In state schools, two thirds of the governors/managers are political appointees. Out of a dozen governors, half will be appointed by the political party currently in power within the local authority; three will represent other parties and three will be co-opted.

An increasing number of boards now have teacher representation and some governing bodies at secondary schools have one or two sixth formers among the members. In the case of further and higher education institutions, governing boards are large (they average twenty-five to thirty members) and include representatives of the teaching and non-teaching staffs, students, the local education authority, industry and commerce and, where appropriate, dons from local universities.

See: Voluntary Schools; School Government.

Graduate Teacher A teacher who holds a degree, either a Bachelor of Education (B.Ed.) or any other degree taken before teacher training. Graduates from universities who wish to enter the teaching profession would normally do an additional year in the university's teacher training department or department of education or go to a college of education or other college of higher education where teacher training is undertaken. Despite the overall growth of the graduate teacher ratio, there is still a severe shortage of graduates in certain fields of teaching. Latest figures (February 1977) indicate that most shortages are in the following subject areas (1976 figures compared with 1975 shortfall figures):

	1975	1976
Mathematics	1582	1859
Physics	345	725

Chemistry	149	168
Gen. Science	245	228
English	932	696
Remedial Edcn.	169	451
Music	219	409
French/German	476	367
Handicraft	382	206
Geography	212	168
Engineering	79	161
Home Economics	131	161

See: Teacher Training; B.Ed. (Bachelor of Education).

Grammar School A secondary school for pupils aged between eleven and eighteen-plus who have been selected for a predominantly academic education with a view to going on to universities or other forms of higher education. Children are selected following an examination taken at the age of eleven-plus (the eleven-plus examination). With the spread in the reorganization to comprehensive education (all-ability, non-selective secondary schools) the grammar school is rapidly disappearing. Most of them were maintained by local education authorities. But more than 170 were direct grant grammar schools, partly financed by the Department of Education and Science. Many of these schools have now already gone or are going fully independent.

Further reading: *The Essential Grammar School* by H. Rée (Harrap, 1956); *Values and Involvement in a Grammar School* by R. King (Routledge and Kegan Paul, 1969); *A Guide to English Schools* by T. Burgess (Penguin, 1969); *Statistics of Education, Vol. 1: Schools* (for statistical background; HMSO annually).

See: Comprehensive Education; Direct Grant Schools; Eleven-plus.

Grants Various forms of financial grants are made for education, ranging from the overall rate support grant, which is made by central government to local authorities to help them finance their schools and further education institutions, to individual grants to students on degree or non-degree courses. The Government also pays grants to the various research bodies, to universities through the University Grants Committee, to direct grant schools (though this form of grant is now being phased out) and to voluntary aided schools and institutions. Grants were introduced by the Local Government Act of 1958, replacing the previous specific grants made in respect of education with the present exchequer aid to local authorities.

But there are other forms of grant aid. For example, a poor parent may apply for a grant to enable his child to stay on at school beyond the statutory leaving age of sixteen, by applying to the local authority for an educational maintenance allowance. Amounts made available vary and parents would be advised to consult their nearest Citizens Advice Bureau for details of how to apply. Special grants may also be claimed for children's uniforms, clothing and meals.

See: Financial Aid; Rate Support Grant; Student Grants; University Grants Committee.

Great Debate National debate on education, which became known as the 'Great Debate', launched in October 1976 by Mr James Callaghan, the Prime Minister, during a speech at the opening of a hall of residence at Ruskin College, Oxford. He called for improved standards in education and the introduction of a core curriculum and urged schools to teach children more about the world of work. This led to a series of regional education conferences chaired by each of the three ministers (including the Secretary of State) for Education in the early months of 1977.

Green Paper Consultative document prepared by the Secretary of State and presented to Parliament. The most recent such document on education was published on 21 July 1977 at the height of the Great Debate on this subject. It was presented to Parliament by Mrs Shirley Williams, Secretary of State for Education and Science, and Mr John Morris, Secretary for Wales. Among its main proposals were:

That local education authorities should carry out a review of curricular arrangements in consultation with the nation's teachers and that their first priority for primary schools should be the formulation of clear aims to achieve basic literacy and numeracy;

That there should be soundly-based means of assessment for individual pupils, for schools and for the education system as a whole;

That schools should encourage parental involvement and local education authorities should provide parents with information about schools and give urgent attention to the problems that can occur when children change schools;

That 'positive discrimination' may be needed to give special help to children who are disadvantaged by social, environmental or other handicaps;

That Certificate of Education courses for student teachers should be phased out and normal minimum entrance qualifications for degree courses for would-be teachers should be raised; in-service training should be extended and a proper induction year for all new teachers introduced; student teachers should be encouraged to work outside the world of education between leaving school and entering training (in order to end the school-college-school syndrome);

That 'extensive consultations' should be undertaken between the Secretary of State and the teachers' unions on how best to remove bad teachers. Adequate warning should be given to teachers 'whose performance is consistently unsatisfactory'; some such teachers might well be moved to more suitable employment;

That local education authorities, schools and industry should work more closely together and that trade unions, industry and commerce should be involved in curriculum planning.

See: School Government.

Group Examination An examination in which a group of subjects is compulsory and must be passed by the candidate if he is to pass the entire examination. The old School Certificate was a group examination, as distinct from the present General Certificate of Education (GCE) which is a subject examination – i.e. candidates may choose from a variety of subjects and pass them one at a time.

See: Examinations.

Gymnasium The German equivalent of the British grammar school. It is thoroughly academic and prepares pupils for higher education and the Abitur examination which acts as a passport to universities. Its equivalent in France is the lycée.

See: Abitur; Lycée.

H

Hadow Reports Sir W. H. Hadow produced three notable reports in the late twenties and early thirties, when he chaired the Consultative Committee of the Board of Education:

Education of the Adolescent (1926) This widened the scope of secondary education and proposed that the school leaving age be raised to fifteen and that secondary education be made available to all. The report, a milestone in educational history, divided education into two main parts: primary, ending at the age of eleven-plus, and secondary, from eleven-plus to fifteen. Secondary schools, it proposed, should be divided into two types: the grammar school, for children of higher ability, and the modern school, for the less able. Children should be able to transfer from one type to the other within the first couple of years.

Primary School Report (1931) This reaffirmed the 1926 proposal to divide primary from secondary education at the age of eleven, and also produced another division: that between infant school and junior school at the age of seven. It recommended that primary school pupils should be allowed to learn through activity and experience, rather than by accumulation of knowledge alone. It proposed that the maximum size of a primary school class should be forty (in many cases it still is).

Infant and Nursery School Report (1933) This report was the first to come out in full support of state-maintained nursery schools from the age of two – an objective which was not to be pursued again until the early seventies, when Mrs Margaret Thatcher, then Education Secretary, made it part of the Conservative party's policy for the immediate future.

Hall of Residence A hostel within or without the campus of a university, college or polytechnic for the students of that institution. Normally it consists of study bedrooms, either single or shared between two, a common room, cooking facilities on each floor, and dining rooms. Many newly-built halls allow students to do their own catering or, alternatively, serve meals in centrally located refectories, which saves money and gives students more freedom and choice. Although halls of residence used to be very strictly single-sex, many colleges and universities have allowed halls to be used by both sexes, usually separated by floors or wings. The cost of accommodation and board, forming part of the student grant, now usually exceeds £300 per year for each student. Prices have risen to such an extent over the past few years that, in a number of cases, students have organized 'rent strikes' – paying what they considered to be the appropriate rent allowance within the grant into a central fund held by the students' union until college authorities negotiated a more reasonable rent. Some of these strikes ended after the authorities threatened to expel students who had not paid rents.

See: Student Grants.

Handicapped Children These are children who suffer from any one of several abnormalities, whether mental, physical or emotional. Special education and special schools are available for the blind, partially sighted, deaf, poor of hearing, physically handicapped, delicate, maladjusted, educationally subnormal, epileptic, those with speech defects and those in hospital. A number of the existing organizations that may be contacted for help and information are listed in the Appendix.

See: Special Education; Special Schools.

Headmasters' Conference (HMC) The association of more than 200 boys' public and direct grant schools, which has met annually as a conference since its foundation in 1869. Headmasters of the schools in membership discuss shared problems. More recently, these problems have been largely concerned with inflation and the increase in the cost of living, and how fees can be kept at a reasonable level. Although these have by tradition been single sex (boys only) schools, many have taken to admitting girls at sixth form level; some, like Bedales and Oakham, are co-educational.

For address to contact, see Appendix.

See: Independent Schools Information Service (ISIS); Independent Schools Joint Council; Girls' Public Day School Trust.

Head Teacher The principal of a school, possessing a fair degree of autonomy in its organization, staffing and curriculum. But he or she is not all-powerful as is often alleged. The head teacher who decides that children should be taught nothing but games and, say, history, will soon find himself confronted by angry managers, governors and parents. Appointed by the local education authority and board of managers/governors, the head is responsible to them.

Further reading: *Headship in the 1970s* by B. Allen (Blackwell, 1970).

Health Education The study of the body and its functions. It is often taken to mean sex education and education in what is now known as 'personal relationships'. But, although such matters are today part and parcel of health education, its purpose is to educate children in personal cleanliness and health, and make them aware of the particular problems caused by smoking, drugs, alcoholism and the like.

Further reading: *The Health of the School Child* (HMSO, 1966); *A Textbook of Health Education* by D. Pirie and A. J. Dalzell-Ward (Tavistock, 1962).

See: Personal Relationships; Sex Education.

Her Majesty's Inspectors (HMI) About 550 inspectors are

attached to the Department of Education and Science to inspect both state-maintained and independent schools to ensure that they are carrying out properly the task of educating the pupils/students in their care. They are civil servants who carry out their duties on behalf of the Secretary of State for Education and Science. They inspect independent schools at appropriate intervals to determine whether these merit (or do not merit) official recognition by the DES, and give advice to teachers, heads and others in the education service on a variety of matters, including curriculum development and examinations. HMI also plan and run courses of in-service training. They should not be confused with local authority inspectors/advisers who are employed, not by the DES, but by the local authority.

See: Educational Advisers.

Higher Education (HE) Post-school education of a kind leading to a degree, diploma or other advanced qualification, usually obtained at a university, polytechnic or college of education. Admission to an institute of higher education normally requires certain minimum entry qualifications at GCE O-level and/or A-level.

Higher Grade See Education in Scotland (Examinations).

Higher National Certificate See HNC.

Higher National Diploma See HND.

Higher School Certificate The advanced part of the School Certificate, similar in structure to the present A-levels. The HSC, normally consisting of two or, at most, three subjects, plus one or two at scholarship level, helped a candidate gain entry to a university. The examination was replaced by the General Certificate of Education (at Ordinary and Advanced levels) in 1951, having first been introduced in 1919.

See: Examinations; School Certificate.

HMC See Headmasters' Conference.

HMI See Her Majesty's Inspectors.

HNC (Higher National Certificate) A widely recognized technical qualification obtained after two years' or more part-time study. To enter, candidates require two A-levels in the General Certificate of Education or an ONC or OND.

See: ONC; OND; HND.

HND (Higher National Diploma) Like the HNC, this offers a qualification in a wide variety of technical and commercial subjects. The HND is of superior standard to the HNC and is reckoned to be the equivalent of a pass degree. Unlike the HNC, ONC and

OND, students studying for the HND are now eligible for a mandatory grant of the kind available for a first degree course. Entry requirements are usually two A-levels and two or three O-levels in the General Certificate of Education, or a good pass in ONC or OND. It requires two years' full-time study or a three-year sandwich course.

See: HNC, ONC; OND; Student Grants.

Holidays According to the 1944 Education Act, schools must be open for 400 sessions, a morning being one session and the afternoon another – hence 200 days per year, five days per week – a total, therefore, of forty weeks. The remainder, twelve weeks, shall be holidays. Such holidays are arranged by the local education authority. An additional period, not exceeding twenty sessions – ten days – may be given at the will of the school managers or governors, and these are normally the half-term breaks or the 'extra half day' normally called for by the guest of honour at speech days or prize-giving ceremonies.

Home Teaching In exceptional circumstances, and with the agreement of the local education authority, some children can be educated full-time at home, either by a qualified tutor or by the child's parent(s). The local authority has to be satisfied that the teaching given is efficient, full-time and in accordance with the child's age, aptitude and ability. In some cases parents have kept their children away from school because they felt it was unsuitable. Such parents would have to subject themselves to a full inspection by the local authority inspectorate. If they do not come up to the required standards, they make themselves liable to prosecution in the courts and could be fined and/or go to prison.

Some parents, because of their geographical position (many miles from a school, working abroad in the jungle or desert, etc.) are able to give children home teaching without too many complications. But if in Britain, they must in all circumstances first win the approval of the local education authority.

Further reading: *The Children on the Hill* by M. Deakin, the riveting story of four children entirely educated at home along Montessori lines (André Deutsch, 1972).

See: Home Tuition; Parents' National Educational Union.

Home Tuition Part-time teaching given by special teachers employed by the local authority to provide suitable education in the home of a child who, for various reasons, does not attend school. Some children might be thus incapacitated through mental or physical handicaps, chronic illness or genuine school phobia. Others might be educated in this way as a result of having been suspended from school because of constant misbehaviour or violence.

Further reading: *The Subnormal Child at Home* by F. J. Schonell, J. A. Richardson and T. S. McConnell (Macmillan, 1958).

Home Visiting Many local authorities, particularly in urban areas, employ special teams of social workers or teachers to visit homes, often in poorer parts of the cities, to help mothers of children under the age of three to improve their understanding of their children through play and verbal communication. The scheme is aimed at giving the mother a more definite role in the development of her child. The same name applies to a system to allow teachers and student teachers to visit homes in order to help them gain a better understanding of the children they teach or are about to teach.

Homework Work set by school for pupils to complete at home and return to their teacher for marking. This is a tricky subject, for the amount of homework given varies from school to school, teacher to teacher. Some schools, particularly most primary schools, set no homework at all. Others are accused of setting too much. Schools cannot insist that a child does homework, which, indirectly, is nothing more than a confession on the part of the school that the curriculum cannot be completely covered during normal school hours. However, it gives the pupil a chance to work on his own and extend his classroom work. Often, the marks given for homework form a reasonable indicator for parents on how well or badly their child is progressing at school. Indeed, it is generally parents who insist that homework be done, rather than teachers. Any parent who believes that a child is being set too much/too little homework, should consult the teacher concerned or the housemaster/year head/head of department. As the pupil nears examinations, the amount of homework generally increases. Parents would be well advised to keep a close watch on the amount of time a child spends on this work. It is not much use if midnight oil has to be burned in order to finish a hefty load of work set by many teachers. It is usually advisable for teachers to produce a homework timetable so that pupils and parents are aware of the subjects to be covered day by day. Three subjects should be a daily limit and, at a rough estimate, between twenty and forty minutes should be spent on each. More than two hours a night should be considered an unnecessary burden for the average child.

Homosexuality Sexual attraction between members of the same sex. The word usually refers to a sexual relationship between two males, while a similar relationship between females is known as lesbianism. It is considered unlawful unless practised by two consenting adults in private. It has been estimated that one male in every twenty is homosexual. Attempts by some teachers to explain to adolescent pupils that such relationships are 'normal' have created hostile controversy in recent years. Discussions of the condition are usually conducted during sex education classes.

See: Sex Education.

Housemaster A teacher who is in charge of a division of a school, called a house. The house is usually given the name of a famous personality or simply a colour (Green House, Blue House). The housemaster acts as one of the head teacher's main representatives and virtually runs his own 'mini school'. In boarding establishments, he also is known as the house father and acts *in loco parentis*.

I

IAPS See Incorporated Association of Preparatory Schools.

Idiot, Imbecile and Moron Three terms used to describe mentally subnormal people. An idiot has an IQ of less than twenty-five, an imbecile has an IQ lying between twenty-five and fifty and a moron has an IQ lying between fifty and seventy-five. Since the 1959 Mental Health Act, the words no longer have legal significance; an idiot is now referred to as severely subnormal, an imbecile as moderately subnormal, a moron as subnormal.

See: Educationally Subnormal (ESN).

ILEA See Inner London Education Authority.

Illiteracy The inability to read or write. The term illiterate is often misused to describe anyone who is simply not very well versed in reading or writing. As a 1950 pamphlet published by the Ministry of Education (*Reading Ability*) put it: 'He is illiterate who is not as literate as someone else thinks he ought to be'. There are certainly those who cannot read or write *at all*; there are also the semi-literate (those who can just about decode words and write falteringly) and those who are only functionally literate, able to read or complete reasonably simple forms and guides but unable to read or comprehend any newspaper more difficult than the popular tabloid dailies.

Further reading: *The Teaching of Reading and Writing* by W. S. Moyle (UNESCO, 1956); *Readability of Newspapers* by D. Moyle and others (Edge Hill College of Education, 1973); *Comparative Reading*, edited by J. Downing (Macmillan, New York, 1973); *A Language for Life* – the Bullock Report (HMSO, 1975).

See: Functional Literacy.

Immigrant Pupils Since the dropping of the ten-year rule, no statistics on immigrant pupils have been collected by the Department of Education and Science and it is becoming increasingly difficult to establish exactly how many immigrant children there are in British schools. Without any clear definition of 'immigrant', it is uncertain whether one is looking at all foreign pupils or all coloured pupils or coloured/foreign pupils with learning difficulties.

Department of Education statistics, kept between 1966 and 1973, were highly unreliable and misleading. Going by the ten-year rule, there were about three hundred thousand immigrant children in Britain in 1972. The figures were dismissed as 'useless' by an all-party Select Committee on Race Relations when it reported in September 1973. The committee estimated that the number of immigrant children needing special help in British schools would grow by about 20,000 a year. There are schools in various parts of the country with more than eighty per cent of their pupils immigrants. It is a problem which, possibly because of its emotive connotations, has been grossly under-researched and mishandled.

Most immigrant children come from Asia and the West Indies (India, Pakistan, Bangladesh, Jamaica in the main). Many of them suffer acute language and other learning difficulties, yet colleges of education and university departments of education almost totally ignore these problems and there are only a handful of courses for teachers of immigrant children (or adults, for that matter).

The Schools Council and the National Foundation for Educational Research have carried out a number of surveys and some projects are in hand.

Further reading: *English for the Children of Immigrants*; Schools Council working paper (HMSO, 1967); *Teaching English to West Indian Children*, Schools Council working paper (Evans-Methuen, 1970); *Multi-racial Education: Need and Innovation*, Schools Council (Evans-Methuen, 1973); *Books for the Multi-racial Classroom* (list) and other books for classroom teaching available from the National

Book League (Address listed in Appendix). *Immigrants at School* by J. Bhatnagar (Cornmarket Press, 1970).

See: Multi-racial Education.

Incorporated Association of Preparatory Schools (IAPS) An organization founded in 1892 following a meeting by about fifty headmasters to discuss the size and weight of the cricket ball to be used by boys at their schools. It now has 455 preparatory schools for boys in membership throughout the British Isles with another 100 abroad. More than 72,000 boys attend the schools. The IAPS, which holds an annual conference, provides a service for parents seeking schools and for staff who seek posts at them. It also runs a joint committee with leaders of industry and commerce to broaden its contacts outside the academic field and organizes training and in-service courses for teachers in preparatory schools.

For address to contact, see Appendix.

See: Preparatory Schools.

Independent Schools Information Service (ISIS) An organization which gives information free of charge to anyone interested in private (independent) schools for boys and girls of all ages. It has some 1100 schools in membership, all recognized as efficient by the Department of Education and Science, and will answer questions about fees, curricula and the like.

ISIS has regional offices in many areas of the country to give advice to parents who wish to find schools in the non-maintained sector for their children. Such regional addresses may be obtained from the organization's national headquarters.

For address to contact, see Appendix.

Independent Schools Joint Advisory Committee (ISJAC) A small committee attached to the Independent Schools Joint Council, which can be called together at short notice to deal with matters of immediate importance.

See: Independent Schools Joint Council (ISJC).

Independent Schools Joint Council (ISJC) A body formed in 1974 as a standing committee to act as spokesman and administrative committee for the independent sector of education as far as any national policy is concerned. It brings together representatives of the various independent schools' associations.

See: Independent Schools Joint Advisory Committee (ISJAC).

Induction Year An improved probation for newly qualified teachers as proposed by the James Report. It allows the new teacher a lighter timetable at school, enabling him or her to spend one fifth of the total time in further training. Guidance and support should be given to the teacher during this year by specially appointed 'professional tutors'. Mrs Shirley Williams, Secretary of State for Education and Science in 1976, allocated special funds to help pay for induction courses for a number of newly qualified teachers.

See: James Report.

Infant School The first division of a primary school, taking in pupils aged between five and seven. About two thirds of such schools form part of primary schools; the remaining third form separate schools.

Initial Teaching Alphabet (ita) Invented by Sir James Pitman (grandson of Sir Isaac Pitman who invented the shorthand system based on phonetics), this alphabet is aimed at simplifying the early stages of learning to read. It consists of forty-four characters, twenty-four of them the same as those included in our normal alphabet and twenty of them new. Together, they form a tightly-knit relationship between the written symbol and the spoken sound. At first suspected and feared, it rapidly gained a solid following both here and in the United States. Those who believed that children would find it difficult to change at a later stage to our traditional orthography were in for a surprise. Children learned reading easily by ita and made the later changeover without difficulty.

For address to contact, see Appendix.

Further reading: *The ita Spelling Guide*; *The ita Instruction Pack*; *The ita Word List* – all available from Initial Teaching Publishing Co. Ltd (address listed in Appendix); *The ita – An Independent Evaluation* by F. W. Warburton and V. Southgate (John Murray/W. & R. Chambers for the Schools Council, 1969); *Evaluating the Initial Teaching Alphabet* by J. Downing (Cassell, 1967); *The ita Symposium* by J. Downing and others (National Foundation for Educational Research, 1967).

See: Pitman, Sir James.

In Loco Parentis A Latin phrase meaning 'in place of the parent'. It is applied to teachers, who have the same legal rights and responsibilities as parents have in the way they treat their pupils. The fact that teachers stand *in loco parentis* has been used as an argument in favour of corporal punishment but parents who claim they never chastise their children might use it as a contrary argument.

Inner London Education Authority (ILEA) The biggest single education authority in the country, it has jurisdiction over about 400,000 pupils in 36 nursery schools, 250 nursery classes attached to primary schools, 870 primary schools (240,000 pupils) and 202 secondary schools (177,000 pupils), 8 further education establishments (56,000 students), 25 colleges, 86 special day schools (9000 pupils), 31 boarding and 6 hospital schools. It is responsible for the education service in twelve inner London boroughs and the City. Its 48-strong education committee with an additional 17 co-opted members is technically part of the Greater London Council established under the London Government Act of 1963 to act as local education authority for the area formerly administered by the London County Council.

See: Local Education Authorities.

In-service Training Training provided for serving teachers, lecturers and others in the educational service for which special leave of absence is given. Courses can be either short or long, the former being run during the school day or in the teachers' own time, either at the school or at teachers' centres. Longer courses are usually organized at colleges of education, university education institutes or polytechnics. They can involve a variety of subjects from modern mathematics to new methods of teaching history or administration for head teachers and heads of departments. Many are planned and run by Her Majesty's Inspectors.

See: Her Majesty's Inspectors (HMI).

Inspectors, Her Majesty's See Her Majesty's Inspectors.

Inspectors, Local Authority See Educational Advisers.

Institutes of Education Institutions that act as a link between colleges of education and the universities. They also contain university departments of education which train graduates in a one-year course to become qualified teachers. They approve the syllabuses of colleges of education, conduct and validate their examinations and provide in-service courses for practising teachers.

See: Colleges of Education; McNair Report.

Integrated Courses These are generally courses at colleges for which apprentices are released by their employers to gain theoretical knowledge and workshop experience. They are full-time courses and very popular with the smaller employer who has neither the money nor the facilities to train apprentices on his own premises.

See: Block Release; Day Release; Sandwich Courses.

Integrated Day An 'untimetabled' day, during which pupils may, either individually or in groups, take part in activities that match their interests. The day could (and often does) stretch into a week or more while children and teachers follow projects involving

not one but several subjects. In fact, subject teaching as such is avoided, the teacher becoming more a guide than an instructor. Activities generally include basic work in language and mathematics.
Integrated Studies Studies of a theme involving various subjects, with individual subject time being surrendered to the study. Teachers normally engaged in special subject areas often unite to work together as a team with groups of pupils. Projects could combine history, geography, written work and mathematics.
Intelligence Quotient (IQ) There are a large number of methods for testing a person's IQ. Briefly, it is the number that compares a child's mental age with his or her chronological age. Thus, if a seven-year-old performs academically like a ten-year-old, his chronological age is seven but his mental age is ten. The average IQ is taken as 100. To calculate the IQ of the seven-year-old, one would divide his mental age by his chronological age and multiply the result by 100:

$$\frac{10}{7} \times 100 = 142.8$$

This child is almost forty-three points above average and would be classified as 'gifted'. On the other hand, a ten-year-old whose academic performance is that of a seven-year-old would have an IQ of:

$$\frac{7}{10} \times 100 = 70$$

This child, who is thirty points below average would be classified as 'backward'. Both categories of children would require (but do not always receive) special education.

Obviously, the child aged seven whose performance is that of a seven-year-old would have an IQ of 100 and would, therefore, be considered 'average'.

IQ tests are generally conducted in verbal reasoning, English and arithmetic. Papers can contain anything up to 100 questions and candidates are given up to forty-five minutes to complete each paper. Younger children (pre-school children for example) can be asked to solve puzzles, such as having to place wooden bricks of varying shapes into trays or 'postboxes' containing holes to take those shapes, or having to copy simple diagrams, etc.

Questions generally begin with problems that are easy to solve and gradually become harder. For example:

Verbal Reasoning Underline the correct answer in the brackets: In is to out as up is to (top, bottom, down, through, hole). If 29384791 means strength, what does 184 mean?

English One word in each sentence below is left unfinished. Write this word in full in the bracket at the side, taking care to spell it correctly.

1. A person who can't hear is d—— (............)
2. Windsor C—— is the home of the Queen (............)
3. Mary took her raincoat in c—— it rained (............)

In each line below, a sentence has been started for you. Write some more words to finish each sentence. The first one has been done for you.

a) Although he disliked *running, he entered every race.*
b) Because of ....
c) Since hearing from........................
d) Crying with.................................

Arithmetic Add: 28, 15, 36. Take 19 from 37 and divide the answer by 6. Write in figures two thousand and twelve. In which of the following numbers does 7 represent the largest quantity? 675; 487; 1578; 710.

Above examples, which are not from actual papers but give a rough idea of the types of questions, are from *A Guide to English Schools* by T. Burgess (Penguin, 1969)

The question absorbing many educational psychologists is whether intelligence is inherited or whether it is developed in accordance with the environment. Sociologists tend to opt for the influence of the environment, while some eminent psychologists believe that genetics play the predominant role in determining one's IQ.

Further reading: *Measurement of Adult Intelligence* by D. Wechsler (Williams & Williams, 1958); *Intelligence and Attainment* by P. E. Vernon (ULP, 1960); *An Introduction to Educational Measurement* by D. Pigeon and A. Yates (Routledge & Kegan Paul, 1969); *The Genetic Determination of Differences in Intelligence* by Sir Cyril Burt (British Journal of Psychology, May 1966, 137–53); *The Psychology of Intelligence* by J. Piaget (Routledge & Kegan Paul, 1950); *The Structure of Human Personality* by H. J. Eysenck (Methuen, 1960); *How Much can we Boost IQ and Scholastic Achievement?* by A. R. Jensen (Harvard Educational Review no. 39, 1969, 1–123); *Inequality* by C. Jencks and others (Allen Lane, The Penguin Press, 1973).

International Baccalauréat (IB) An examination giving the successful candidate admission to universities throughout the world. More than 400 universities, including all British universities, accept the IB as a valid entrance qualification. It has been reported that some 6000 students who offered the IB for entry have so far been successful in taking their degrees, and that of the first fifty students who entered British universities with the IB and graduated in 1976, six obtained first class degrees. The IB is taken at a large number of schools, particularly the International Schools and Colleges. In Britain, these include the United World College of the Atlantic, South Wales, and West London College. From September 1977, the IB has also been offered by Avery Hill College, London, to students who have already gained a minimum of five O-levels.

Candidates are examined in six subjects, three of them at higher and three at subsidiary level. Marking is along a seven-point scale (1 = very poor, 7 = excellent, 4 = satisfactory). A candidate who fails because of insufficient marks in one subject may take that subject again without loss of marks in the other five subjects. If he fails again, he loses all marks and must take the examination again.

In general, the six-subject scheme comprises: first language, including a syllabus for world literature in translation; second language; study of man, made up of a number of options, including history, geography, economics, philosophy; sciences, with options including physics, chemistry, biology; mathematics; one of a number of options including arts, music, an ancient language or an option not already chosen from the third or fourth categories above.

For address to contact, see Appendix.

Further reading: *The International Baccalauréat* by A. D. C. Peterson (Harrap, 1972).

International Bureau of Education (IBE) Founded in Geneva in 1925 as an inter-governmental organization for educational research and dissemination of information. It organizes annual conferences in conjunction with UNESCO to debate educational problems, such as literacy, curricula, education for life, etc. These conferences are attended by the Ministers of Education or their representatives from some eighty nations. It publishes numerous documents and journals in English and French, including reports on comparative education and bibliographies.

For address to contact, see Appendix.

See: UNESCO.

IQ See Intelligence Quotient.

ISIS See Independent Schools Information Service.

ISJAC See Independent Schools Joint Advisory Committee.
ita See Initial Teaching Alphabet.

J

James Committee A committee set up by Mrs Margaret Thatcher in November 1970, while she was Secretary of State for Education and Science, to look into the education, training and probation of teachers in England and Wales, the content of teacher training courses, and the role of the colleges of education, universities and polytechnics in teacher supply and training. Under the chairmanship of Lord James of Rusholme (former High Master of Manchester Grammar School and Vice-Chancellor of York University), it published its controversial report *Teacher Education and Training* (HMSO) in 1972 and provided a major contribution to Mrs Thatcher's White Paper (Cmnd 5174) also published that year as *Education: A Framework for Expansion*. It was this White Paper which paved the way for the expansion of polytechnics, the establishment of regional committees to co-ordinate the education and training of teachers and the introduction of the Diploma in Higher Education (Dip.H.E.), a new two-year course which could be used as a terminal qualification or as a stepping stone to the Bachelor of Education (B.Ed.) degree.

Jewish Lecture Committee The section within the Board of Deputies of British Jews, which supplies speakers on Judaism and conducts studies on Jewish education and race relations. The committee, set up in 1933, provides teacher notes on Jewish religious education as well as films and film strips on Israel, Jewish festivals, the synagogue and other related matters.

For address to contact, see Appendix.

Joint Four Four separate teachers' associations that have a joint interest and, therefore, a joint executive. The four are: the Association of Headmistresses (AHM), the Headmasters' Association (HMA), the Association of Assistant Mistresses (AAM) and the Assistant Masters' Association (AMA). Members are almost invariably in secondary schools.

See: AMA; Association of Headmistresses.

Junior School The senior division of a primary school, attended by children from the age of seven up to the age of eleven-plus, when they enter secondary school, or until eight or nine, when they enter a middle school. Most primary schools have both infant and junior departments and some have nursery classes attached.

See: Infant School; Primary School.

Junior Training Centres These are institutions for severely subnormal children (formerly known in legal terms as idiots). Through great patience and highly dedicated teachers, children once labelled as ineducable are taught in these centres, often by Montessori methods. They learn some of the basic essentials of living, such as the tying of shoe-laces, the use of a knife and fork, the recognition of shapes and colours.

See: Idiot, Imbecile and Moron; Montessori Methods.

Juvenile Court Children aged between ten and seventeen may be brought before a juvenile court if they are considered to have committed an offence against the law. Lay magistrates, often with experience in dealing with children, will hear cases brought to the court by the police or by the council. Such cases need not be of alleged criminal offences, but could involve the belief that the child is in need of care and protection. The magistrate may reject an application regarding the child by a council; order parents to take proper care and exercise proper control over the child; make a supervision order so that the child is regularly watched by a probation officer or social worker; or make a care order, which will place the child in a community home or other residential place away from his own home. Fines and other penalties may also be imposed. A child under the age of ten may not be brought to the court for an alleged offence, but may appear if it is believed the child is in need of care and protection.

See: Community Homes.

K

Kindergarten A school or class for young children, usually from three to five years old, that prepares children for compulsory schooling, helping them learn through play and discovery. The name was coined by Friedrich Froebel and is the German for 'children's garden'. Such schools are better known in Britain as nursery schools.

See: Froebel, Friedrich; Nursery School.

L

Language Laboratory This is a classroom fitted out with a series of booths, each containing a tape recorder, microphone and taped lesson to which a pupil may listen through earphones. The tape is linked to a centralized console, which allows the teacher to tune in to any of the lessons being followed. Pupils repeat phrases or answer questions posed either on the tape or by the teacher, who can interrupt from the console without disturbing any of the other pupils. There are several advantages of this method. The pupil is able to work at his own speed and ability and can obtain personal tuition as opposed to being part of a large classroom lesson. Moreover, many different lessons and/or languages may be taught simultaneously, at varying levels of difficulty. Among the disadvantages (apart from the expense of the equipment) are the facts that teachers do not always listen in at the point when their help is most needed and that children often fail to take advantage of the system.

Further reading: *The Language Laboratory in School* by J. B. Hilton (Methuen, 1966).

Late Developer Not all children develop their abilities at the same rate. Some are slower or quicker than others. The late developer is a child who appears to have become stuck in a learning groove and finds himself falling behind other pupils in his class. Later, the same child might suddenly grasp what in the past had been ungraspable and not only catch up the average pupils in the class but even surpass them. It is often difficult to know when a child is a late developer and when he is genuinely backward. Often, the late developer becomes stuck on just one or two subjects, yet makes reasonable headway in others. Great patience, both by teachers and parents, is required here.

LEA See Local Education Authorities.

Leaving Age See School Leaving Age.

Leicestershire Plan A scheme whereby pupils are transferred from primary schools to a junior comprehensive school at the age of eleven-plus and remain there until the statutory leaving age or are moved at thirteen or fourteen, at the request of the parent, to a grammar school where they will take the GCE O and A-level examinations or the Certificate of Secondary Education (CSE). This plan was first introduced in the county of Leicestershire in 1957 in order to reorganize secondary education without too much pain (or money) and to prevent the establishment of big, possibly unmanageable comprehensives.

Further reading: *The Leicestershire Experiment* by S. C. Mason (Councils and Education Press, 1957).

See: Comprehensive Education.

Liberal Studies Groups of subjects that have been designed to broaden the outlook of students who specialize in technological or science sectors for a vocational purpose. Nowadays, almost all subjects can be listed under the heading of liberal studies and the student may pick from a wealth of options. These could include courses on the arts or/and the humanities, or they could involve a study of political and social sciences (although these subjects are not, of course, exact sciences), the trade union movement, or even vague course-titles, such as 'Man's role in society' or 'The role of the mass media in the contemporary world'.

Linked Courses Since 1971, school courses have in many cases been so designed that pupils in the senior classes, can undertake part of them at local colleges of further education. Most of such courses are vocational, such as commerce, engineering, applied science, catering or building. The purpose behind the idea is to give sixth formers a practical introduction to continuing general education and allow them to mix with more adult students.

List 99 This is the 'black list' kept by the Department of Education and Science on which the names of teachers considered unsuitable for employment in schools and colleges are recorded. It is a highly confidential register, which has given rise to considerable concern among teaching unions, who consider it an intrusion into civil liberty. In 1977, the list contained in the region of 1200 names. These names are of teachers who have been dismissed on one of the few grounds possible for such action: sexual relations with a pupil or pupils of the same or opposite sex; conviction in a civil court of law on a criminal charge; gross misconduct detrimental to the profession, such as the theft of school funds or similar misdemeanours.

Teachers so listed may appeal 'at some future date' for their names to be removed from the list. A few – about a dozen – names are removed from the list annually.

Further reading: *List 99* by Peter Smith (*AMA*, Journal of the Assistant Masters' Association, Vol. 72, No. 1, January 1977).

Local Teacher Associations These are union branches. Local associations throughout the country are often grouped into regions or metropolitan divisions (e.g. associations within Greater Manchester, Derbyshire and Nottinghamshire, West Midlands, etc.).

For individual associations, names of association (branch) secretaries and their addresses, contact either the union or see details in *Educational Committees Year Book*, published annually by Councils and Education Press (address listed in Appendix).

Local Education Authorities (LEAs) The Education Act of 1944 made the county boroughs and counties into local education authorities with responsibility for the education in schools and colleges within their boundaries. It deprived county districts of their responsibility for education. Each LEA had its chief education officer or director of education, a public employee, together with his team of assistants and school inspectors, or advisers, medical officers, educational psychologists, etc. Each was politically run by an education committee, elected by local ratepayers. Until April 1974 there were 162 LEAs in England and Wales, while in Scotland there were thirty-five such authorities until May 1975.

Local Government reorganization radically changed the face of the authorities and areas, cutting their number in England and Wales from 162 to 104 and in Scotland from thirty-five to twelve. Northern Ireland has five Education and Library Boards.

The 104 are divided into thirty-six metropolitan districts, forty-seven non-metropolitan counties (eight of them in Wales) and twenty-one London boroughs (including ILEA).

The twelve Scottish authorities are made up of nine regional education authorities and three island area education authorities.

As a result of this 'rationalization', many education officers were forced to resign or retire early and the political face of some areas was changed. The demise also of divisional executives and excepted districts brought additional power to local education authorities which brought chief executives to the top of the administration tree.

Before reorganization, two counties and thirty county boroughs had a population of fewer than 100,000. Today, the smallest county is the Isle of Wight with a population of 110,000. The London borough of Kingston has a 139,000-strong population and is the second smallest in the country. Barking, another London borough, follows with 158,000 and South Tyneside metropolitan district comes next with 173,000. The Inner London Education Authority remains the biggest single authority with 2,650,000.

Authorities are powerful and, apart from their dependence on money allocations from central Government, are autonomous in the way they run their educational establishments. The 1976 Education Act took away some of that autonomy in that the Government sought to force all LEAs to go fully comprehensive in their secondary school reorganization.

Further reading: *Local Government and Education* by D. E. Regan (George Allen and Unwin, 1977).

See: Educational Administration; Education Committee.

London Allowance A special weighting bonus given to about 112,000 teachers in the Greater London area, including those in further education, to make up for the additional cost of living in and around the capital. Before the Houghton Report (December 1974) the allowance was paid only to teachers in Inner London and the Outer London boroughs. Houghton added a third fringe tier to take in teachers beyond the Outer London boundaries.

The allowance from April 1975 was and still remains: Inner London: £402 p.a. or an extra £7.73 a week; Outer London: £297 (£5.71); fringe areas: £150 (£2.88).

Lycée French selective school, similar to the British grammar school and the German Gymnasium. It is of a highly academic character and leads its pupils to the Baccalauréat examination which admits them to universities.

See: Baccalauréat.

M

McNair Report In 1944, a committee was set up under the chairmanship of Sir Arnold McNair to consider the supply, recruitment and training of teachers and youth leaders. It recommended the raising of teacher status and the recruitment of would-be teachers from a wider field, that teacher salaries be increased and that the Burnham Committee should have a single negotiating body for both primary and secondary school teachers. It also proposed, against some opposition, the setting up of institutes or schools of education to form a link between teacher training colleges and universities, such institutes to be responsible for the co-ordination of teacher training in their area.

See: Colleges of Education; Institutes of Education.

Managers See Governors and Managers, Board of.

Mandatory Grants See Student Grants.

Matriculation Candidates who took the School Certificate and obtained five subjects at credit grade, including English, mathematics or a science subject, and one foreign language, were said to have matriculated for university purposes. This exempted them from having to pass a first year's foundation course at a university. The present Ordinary level examination of the General Certificate of Education has replaced the School Certificate and single-subject passes are considered equivalent to the School Certificate subject credits.

See: Examinations; School Certificate.

Mature State Scholarship Awards made annually by the Department of Education and Science to students aged 25-plus who have been attending adult education courses and show themselves willing and able to enter a university for a degree course but who missed their opportunity of doing do at the more usual age of 18-plus

For address to contact, see Appendix.

See: Mature Students.

Mature Students Those students who return to study at a higher academic level, either to take degrees or to become teachers. The term mature student refers to age rather than to ability, although it has been generally found that such students are often more dedicated and tend to do well. Some colleges of education specialize in taking mature students, and a few universities, particularly Sussex, have special rules of admission for older students (usually aged 25-plus) who have shown that they might well be capable of tackling and passing a degree course without necessarily having the usual qualifications for university entry (A-levels or their equivalent). The Open University is the prime example of an institution of higher education which accepts students without previous qualifications.

See: Open University.

Medical Inspection All schools maintained by the state must provide facilities for medical inspections to be carried out by the local authority-appointed medical officer and his team. Department of Education Regulations demand that inspections take place soon after the child's admission to an infants' school, again in the last year of primary education, and in the final year of secondary education. Other inspections may be conducted as and when it is deemed necessary. Parents may ask to attend such inspections and are usually welcome.

Mentally Handicapped Children Such children, on account of their brain dysfunction, suffer great difficulties in learning. The type of education available to mentally handicapped children depends on the severity of the handicap. Some children require special education in hospital schools, others may attend normal schools and profit from them.

For address to contact, see Appendix.

See: Educationally Subnormal; Idiot, Imbecile and Moron; Junior Training Centres; Special Education.

Middle School A school that first appeared in the late sixties as one that would ease the transition of children from the more traditional primary schools to comprehensives. It caters for children aged from eight to twelve or nine to thirteen, though there are some which take pupils aged from nine to twelve, and from ten to thirteen. These schools are growing in popularity and almost every local authority now has some. They were first proposed in *Children and their Primary Schools*, published in 1967 and better known as the Plowden Report, although some already existed at that time, following the 1964 Education Act, which allowed local authorities to vary the transfer age of pupils from primary to secondary schools.

Further reading: *The Middle Years of Schooling from 8 to 13*, Schools Council Working Paper no. 22 (HMSO, 1969); *Education in the Middle Years* by A. M. Ross and others, Schools Council Working Paper no. 42 (Evans-Methuen Educational, 1972); *Towards the Middle School*, DES pamphlet no. 57 (HMSO, 1970); *The Middle School System*, a survey by the Assistant Masters' Association (AMA, 1976).

See: Comprehensive Education; Plowden Report.

Milk The 1944 Education Act made it the duty of local authorities to provide all children in school with free milk and this was the case until 1968. In September of that year, the Labour Government withdrew the free one third of a pint every child received daily in secondary schools. It was one of the victims of the Government's economy measures. Primary schools continued to receive it until September 1971, when another economy measure – this time ordered by a Conservative Government – withdrew it from children in junior schools – i.e. from the age of seven-plus. Those in nursery and infant schools (aged from three to seven) continue to receive the free one third pint daily. Those aged between seven and eleven receive it only if a medical examination shows that they are in need of it. Those in special schools also continue to receive it.

Minister of State The Secretary of State for Education and Science is given two or three MPs to assist him or her. They are called under-Secretaries of State or Junior Ministers, but can be given a senior position as Minister of State for Education. This gives the holder a higher status and places him between the under-Secretary and the Secretary of State. Ministers have responsibilities delegated to them by the Secretary of State; thus, one will be delegated to deal with schools, another with further and higher education, another with the arts.

See: Ministers of Education; Secretary of State.

Ministers of Education The following is a list of those who have been in charge of British education since the beginning of the century.

Presidents of the Board of Education (1900–44)

Duke of Devonshire (Spencer Compton) (1900–2)
Marquess of Londonderry (Charles Steward) (1902–5)
Mr Augustine Birrell (1905–7)
Mr Reginald McKenna (1907–8)
Mr Walter Runciman (1908–11)
Mr Joseph Pease (1911–15)
Mr Arthur Henderson (1915–16)
Marquess of Crewe (1916)
Mr Herbert Fisher (1916–22)
Mr E. F. L. Wood (1922–4)
Mr Charles Trevelyan (1924)
Lord Eustace Percy (1924–9)
Sir Charles Trevelyan (formerly C. P. Trevelyan) (1929–31)
Mr H. B. Lees-Smith (1931)
Sir Donald Maclean (1931–2)
Lord Irwin (1932–5)
Mr Oliver Stanley (1935–7)
Mr Karl Stanhope (1937–8)
Lord de la Warr (1938–40)
Mr H. Ramsbotham (1940–1)
Mr R. A. Butler (1941–5)

It was during R. A. Butler's term of office that the 1944 Education Act was passed and the Board of Education became the Ministry of Education.

Ministers of Education (1944–64)

Mr R. K. Law (1945)

Miss Ellen Wilkinson (1945–7)

Mr George Tomlinson
(1947–51)

Miss Florence Horsbrugh
(1951–4)

Sir David Eccles (1954–7)

Lord Hailsham (1957)

Mr Geoffrey Lloyd (1957–9)

Sir David Eccles (1959–62)

Sir Edward Boyle (1962–4)

On 1 April 1964, the Ministry of Education was renamed the Department of Education and Science.

Secretaries of State, Department of Education and Science (from 1964)

Mr Quintin Hogg (formerly
Lord Hailsham) (1964)

Mr Michael Stewart (1964–5)

Mr Anthony Crosland (1965–7)

Mr Patrick Gordon Walker
(1967–8)

Mr Edward Short (1968–70)

Mrs Margaret Thatcher
(1970–4)

Mr Reginald Prentice (1974–5)

Mr Frederick Mulley (1975–6)

Mrs Shirley Williams (1976–   )

Modern Languages These are languages taught second to English in schools and universities, such as French, German, Spanish, Russian and Italian. Although French is by far the most popular in secondary schools, and is already taught to juniors at some primary schools, it is fast becoming a shortage subject, with too few teachers qualified in the subject. German is rapidly joining Latin and Greek as a minority subject and Spanish is almost non-existent as far as candidates for A-level are concerned. Britain has always been reputed to be a nation of 'lazy linguists'. Her membership of the Common Market has done nothing to rectify this view. Even successful A-level candidates in French, German and Spanish may fail to speak such languages properly – i.e. with a correct accent – for the simple reason that they are taught in English. There are now moves afoot to require all modern language teachers to spend at least one term in every seven years in the country where the language they are teaching is spoken.

Modern Mathematics The introduction of a modern mathematics syllabus into schools was supposed to allow children to understand the basic concepts of the subject, moving emphasis away from the mere facility in the manipulation of numbers (multiplication, division, etc.) or from the familiar geometry of Euclid. To some extent the content of a modern syllabus reflects the change in outlook which has occurred in mathematics since the late nineteenth century. Thus recurring patterns and unifying structures are sought. However, less time is spent doing routine calculations which are necessary for the practical applications of mathematics at work (this is increasingly the case with the advent of the cheap pocket calculator, which may now be used even in examinations). Perhaps the weakness of the modern approach to mathematics teaching is that it takes numerical calculation as a routine procedure (which, strictly speaking, it is, as a calculator will show).

Unless taught by teachers who have themselves been well grounded in modern mathematics, this method could become counterproductive. Poor teaching has tended to confuse children even more and employers as well as universities have complained that school leavers and undergraduates have lower standards in mathematics than ever before. It has also been established by some educationists that modern mathematics, even when in the hands of good teachers, is comprehensible only to the brighter pupil and that the less bright find it hard to cope with the method.

Modes 1-3 There are three different 'modes' of examining. Mode 1, perhaps the most familiar, is where an examining board sets or prescribes a syllabus for schools and bases its examination on that syllabus. Such examinations are also marked by external examiners appointed by the board. Mode 3, usually adopted for the Certificate of Secondary Education (CSE), is an examination based on a syllabus chosen by the teachers themselves and marked by them but moderated by external examiners. Mode 2 is the system which falls between these two methods, giving schools a choice of either or a mixture of both.

See: Examinations.

Monitor The prefectoral system applied to the more junior classes: pupils who have been assigned certain tasks to help teachers and the smooth running of the class, such as the cleaning of blackboards ('blackboard monitor') or the handing out of books and even to a certain extent, the keeping of order when a teacher is out of the room.

See: Prefects.

Montessori Method A system of teaching young children, which emphasizes training of the senses and guidance, rather than rigid control, of the child's activity so as to encourage self-education. It was developed by Maria Montessori (1870–1952), the first Italian woman to qualify as a doctor of medicine in Italy (1894). Her first school was opened in Rome in 1907 and here she encouraged the use of games and toys to keep children active and help them discover knowledge for themselves. Her ideas spread and similar schools were opened in Europe and the United States. Her school was closed in 1934 by Mussolini and she fled to Spain.

Further reading: *Maria Montessori* by E. M. Standing (Hollis and Carter, 1957); *The Secret of Childhood* by Maria Montessori, translated from the Italian (Longmans, 1936); *The Children on the Hill* by M. Deakin (André Deutsch, 1972).

See: Discovery Methods.

Moron See Idiot, Imbecile and Moron.

Multilateral School This was an attempt to create a version of a comprehensive school by placing all three types of school (grammar, secondary modern and technical) under the same roof, yet kept apart in separate sections. In Germany, where they are still experimenting with comprehensive education, this type of school is called a co-operative school, which is a fair description but a poor excuse for what is meant to be an all-ability comprehensive.

See: Comprehensive Education; Bilateral School.

Multi-racial Education Lessons or textbooks for use in lessons aimed at racially mixed classes. A number of bodies try to further the interests of children in such situations and to help and advise teachers. They include the Community Relations Commission which publishes a monthly newsletter, *Education and Community Relations*, as well as an informative quarterly journal, *Ethnic Minorities and Employment*, and the National Association for Multi-racial Education (NAME), which publishes a newsletter each term called *Multi-racial School* and many information pamphlets.

For addresses to contact, see Appendix.

See: Immigrant Pupils.

Music Education Music, one of the most important subjects in the educational development of the child, has made massive strides over the past two decades. At one time, music meant a weekly lesson in choir singing in the school hall. The luckier ones managed to scrape together a few recorders and perhaps a scratchy violin or two. Today, many instruments are taught to all children with talent and interest, but they also learn to read and write music, to appreciate sound, whether popular or classical. A few schools specialize in music teaching, including state-maintained comprehensive schools. Possibly the most famous of the independents in this field is Chetham's

Hospital School of Music in Manchester, a non-denominational, co-educational school which admits talented youngsters from the age of seven. There are also a number of colleges of music with high reputations.

For addresses to contact, see Appendix.

N

National Association of Head Teachers (NAHT) Founded in 1897 to bring together on a national basis the various head teacher associations that had existed over many years in England and Wales. Its membership now exceeds 19,000 and represents about two-thirds of all maintained primary and secondary school heads in the country. As such it claims to be the largest single body of heads in Europe. Its constitution sets out the aims of the association: to provide a ready means of communication for and giving expression to the opinions of all head teachers, to act for and on behalf of its members and to help those in professional or legal difficulties. It also seeks to uphold high standards among head teachers and to promote and further the cause of education in general.

Like most other teacher unions, it is represented on the Burnham Committee, but is fighting to have the salaries of head teachers negotiated separately from those of assistant teachers. It also wants to set up a General Teaching Council (or Teachers General Council) to give the profession some degree of self government and to act as a watchdog over teaching status and standards.

For address to contact, see Appendix.

National Association of Inspectors and Educational Advisers (NAIEA) An organization representing more than 900 out of the total 1450 inspectors in local authority service. Each local authority inspector covers about 25 schools and 420 teachers. Local inspectors are sometimes called advisers. But inspectors advise and advisers inspect and there has often been confusion about these roles. The association considers its members to be the servants of both schools and local authorities.

For address to contact, see Appendix.

National Association of Schoolmasters/Union of Women

Teachers (NAS/UWT) Founded in 1919 by male teachers working in England and Wales who felt themselves unable to go along with the policies of the bigger National Union of Teachers. For more than half a century, the NAS was considered a misogynous organization as well as a militant one. It was not until 1 January 1976 that the NAS merged with the comparatively recently founded Union of Women Teachers and the Scottish Schoolmasters' Association to become the NAS/UWT, whose combined membership totals more than 90,000, making it the second biggest association of teachers in the country. Its aims are to make teaching an attractive career for well qualified men and women and it has fought for salaries that would equal those in comparable professions, such as the Civil Service. It is affiliated to the TUC and is intent on securing the formation of a Teachers General Council to give the profession some degree of self government.

It has its own residential education centre (at Rednal, near Birmingham) where it runs professional courses for its members and trains its local officers and school representatives in the art of negotiating for better conditions. It has played an active part in developing the role of British teachers within the European Common Market though the European Teachers Trade Union Committee (ETTUC) and is also affiliated to the International Federation of Free Teachers' Unions (IFFTU).

For address to contact, see Appendix.

National Association of Teachers in Further and Higher Education (NATFHE) A union formed in January 1976 following the merger between the Association of Teachers in Colleges and Departments of Education (ATCDE, founded 1943) and the Association of Teachers in Technical Institutions (ATTI, founded 1904), with a total membership of 63,000 – about eighty-five per cent of teachers in polytechnics, colleges of education, institutes of higher education, colleges of technology, colleges of further education, colleges of art, colleges of agriculture and in adult education. It is a union whose aim is to protect the professional interests of its members and it holds an annual conference. It is represented on the Burnham Committee, the Schools Council and is affiliated to the TUC.

National Extension College Non-profitmaking correspondence college, founded in 1963 by the Advisory Centre of Education (ACE). A year later, the NEC launched the College of the Air, the first link between correspondence schools and British television. Courses range from those for beginners who want to see if they could profit from correspondence education to GCE O and A-level courses as well as the Gateway courses for the Open University and London University external degrees. It publishes a free newsletter, *Home Study*, four times a year, which advises on the improvement of study techniques, and provides facilities for face-to-face discussions between tutors and students.

For address to contact, see Appendix.

See: Advisory Centre for Education; Open University.

National Foundation for Educational Research (NFER) A body funded by the Government and local education authorities to carry out research into all areas of education, including educational psychology, the teaching of reading, writing and arithmetic, the teaching of French in primary schools, the effects of streaming, the organization and reorganization of secondary schools into comprehensives, immigrant education, the learning of English by foreigners and many other fields. It often works in close collaboration with the Schools Council. It produces an annual report and a journal, *Educational Research*.

For address to contact, see Appendix.

National Institute of Adult Education (NIAE) A national reference centre for all kinds of adult education. Formed in 1921, it has a governing council with representatives from the various local authority associations, the universities, the Armed Forces, the Home Office, the Department of Education and Science and numerous voluntary bodies, such as the Workers' Educational Association (WEA). It publishes a number of journals, including the bi-monthly *Adult Education* and the quarterly *Teaching Adults*. It holds annual conferences.

For address to contact, see Appendix.

Further reading: *Year Book of Adult Education* (NIAE, every September); *Research in Adult Education in the British Isles* (NIAE); *Select Bibliography of Adult Education in Great Britain* (NIAE); *A History of Adult Education in Great Britain* by T. Kelly (Liverpool University Press, 1962).

See: Adult Education; Workers' Educational Association; Scottish Institute of Adult Education.

National Listening Library A registered charity founded in 1972 to provide a postal service of 'talking books' for the handicapped, including spastics and those suffering from polio, muscular dystrophy, multiple sclerosis, spina bifida or rheumatoid arthritis, or who are old or frail, or are partially sighted or dyslexic.

For address to contact, see Appendix.

National Nursery Examination Board A body which awards certificates to properly trained nursery school assistants. A nursery school must be staffed by one certificated teacher with special training in nursery work, and a full-time asssitant holding the Board's certificate for every twenty full-time children in it. A nursery class attached to a primary school needs the same staff but for every thirty full-time children.

For address to contact, see Appendix.

See: Nursery Class; Nursery Nurse; Nursery School.

National Union of School Students (NUSS) This union evolved in the early to mid-seventies out of growing campaigns by pupils, particularly radical sixth formers, against corporal punishment, the wearing of school uniforms, examinations, etc. The NUSS wants pupils to be given the right to participate in the decision-making within their own schools, seeking (and in some areas actually getting) places on the governing boards of secondary schools. The union is closely affiliated to the National Union of Students, which gives practical help and advice, and has the use of an office in NUS London headquarters. It claims to have 10,000 members, but this is likely to be an exaggeration.

For address to contact, see Appendix.

See: Schools Action Union

National Union of Students (NUS) The NUS, founded in 1922, now has nearly 800,000 members in about 700 colleges, polytechnics, universities and other educational institutions. It represents their interests both at local and at national level and its leaders negotiate with the Department of Education and Science for increases in student grants and improved conditions. It also acts as a strong pressure group on all kinds of issues, whether educational or political, organizing mass demonstrations at universities and in towns and cities, in protest against or in favour of a variety of matters, from grants and the (more recent) Government financial cuts in education, to abortion law reforms and women's liberation. Run by an executive committee, which has for some years been left-wing in character, its aims have often been radical. Its president and officers are elected by representatives of the affiliated local student unions who meet at a national conference twice a year. Until 1976–7, the union had a number of excellent service companies, including NUS Travel Ltd and two printing companies, which went into liquidation following heavy financial losses, and an insurance company (Endsleigh

Insurance) which had to be sold, but which continues to organize student insurance and has always been profitable. Local college unions pay small *per capita* affiliation fees to the NUS in return for its services.

For address to contact, see Appendix.

See: Scottish Union of Students (SUS).

National Union of Teachers See NUT.

New Sixth See Examinations (Certificate of Extended Education).

Newsom Reports Two committees set up by the Government under the chairmanship of Sir John Newsom produced reports of far-reaching consequences. The first, possibly the more famous of the two, became known as the Newsom Report (1963). It was called *Half Our Future* and dealt with the education of pupils of average or below average ability, aged between thirteen and sixteen. It recommended the raising of the school leaving age from fifteen to sixteen as of 1965 (this was later postponed due to economic circumstances); the payment of special bonuses to teachers who were prepared to teach in schools in problem areas; special curricula for the less able pupils to prepare them for the outside world; a revision of the agreed syllabus for religious education; better sexual instruction for adolescents; the provision of audio-visual equipment to all secondary schools; better school building programmes and the improvement of poor, old buildings.

The other Newsom-chaired committee produced the first of a two-part report on public schools (Public Schools Commission). It appeared in 1968 and recommended that 38,000 pupils in need of boarding education should be admitted by public (boarding) schools and should be paid for either by the Government or by local authorities.

See: School Leaving Age.

Nursery Class A class attached to a primary school for children aged from three to five. By law, such classes must not have more than thirty children in them.

See: Nursery School.

Nursery Nurse A trained person with a certificate from the National Nursery Examining Board, which qualifies the holder to help teachers in nursery schools or classes.

See: National Nursery Examining Board.

Nursery School A school for children aged from three to five (some admit toddlers aged two) which prepares them for compulsory schooling. By law, classes must not have more than thirty children in them. At present, approximately 30,000 children are attending 580 nursery schools.

See: Kindergarten; Nursery Class.

NUS See National Union of Students.

NUSS See National Union of School Students.

NUT (National Union of Teachers) This is by far the biggest single professional organization for teachers and it is among the most influential. It holds the overall majority in the Burnham Committee and, therefore, is regarded as the union that controls teacher salaries. It is affiliated to the TUC and since the late sixties has become one of the most militant and campaigning teacher-bodies Because it was originally known as the National Union of Elementary Teachers when it was founded in 1870 with just 400 members in 26 local associations, it is even now still regarded as being essentially an organization of primary school teachers. It dropped the title for the more comprehensive NUT in 1888 after it had gained wider support and now has more than 284,000 members. Of these, 220,000 are serving teachers in every kind of school. Of the remainder, about 47,000 are associate members studying to become teachers in colleges of education and some 18,000 are members who have left the profession, usually through retirement, but who keep a close contact with the union.

Its aims are to advance the status, conditions and salaries of the teaching profession and to improve educational standards. It provides legal assistance, insurance facilities and professional help to its members.

It has an executive committee of forty-four, which meets regularly, and holds an annual conference (at Easter) attended by some 2000 delegates. Its general secretary is a member of the TUC General Council.

Subscriptions differ according to whether members are associate, newly qualified or have served one, two or more years. Until the end of 1975, an allocation of ten per cent of the subscription income went to the union's sustentation fund. This was discontinued from January 1976 (when the fund stood at about £4 million) and is subject to annual review.

For information about membership, subscription, services and policies, contact address listed in Appendix.

See: AMA (Assistant Masters' Association).

O

O-level The Ordinary level examination in the General Certificate of Education (GCE), which replaced the School Certificate in 1952 and was to give children a 'reasonable test' in any given subject they had learned at secondary school. Normally taken at the age of sixteen, it is roughly equivalent to the credit grade of subjects once taken in the School Certificate. Subjects may be taken singly and certificates are awarded for one or more O-levels. It acts as an entry qualification to numerous professions and for university matriculation. Most employers require candidates to show proof of having passed one or more examinations at this level, but the Schools Council has recommended scrapping O-levels and the Certificate of Secondary Education (CSE) and replacing them with a single system of examining by 1981. The Council was instructed in 1976 by the DES to carry out more research and feasibility studies on such a new examination before it would be given the official go-ahead. Parents and employers, as well as some teachers, were opposed to another change in the examination system.

See: Examinations; Matriculation.

ONC (Ordinary National Certificate) This qualification is of about the same standard as the A-level in the GCE and is awarded after two years of part-time study in a variety of (usually technical) subjects at technical or further education colleges. To be admitted to such a course, the candidate would normally require four O-levels in the GCE or their equivalents (e.g. four grade 1 passes in the CSE).

See: Examinations; OND.

OND (Ordinary National Diploma) Like the ONC, this qualification is of about the same standard as the A-level in the GCE. It is awarded after two years of full-time study or a sandwich course, and a pass of a high standard could enable the holder to enter a university or polytechnic for a degree or other higher course. To enter such a course, the candidate would normally require four O-levels or their equivalent (e.g. four grade 1 passes in the CSE).

See: Examinations; ONC.

Open University An institution set up by Royal Charter to provide higher education by 'distance study' – i.e. study at home by correspondence courses, leading to a degree. Radio and television programmes supplement printed material and there are numerous tuition centres throughout the country where students may meet tutors. All students must attend a summer course, which normally lasts two weeks and is held at one of the conventional universities, often the university nearest to the student. The first students enrolled for courses in 1971 (the academic year starts in January) and thousands have already graduated with full degrees awarded by the University. Most students are aged twenty-one and over (some are octogenarians), though students aged 18-plus were admitted in limited numbers (500) for a (not altogether successful) experiment. More than 40,000 students are on its rolls. Tuition fees, books and summer course fees are paid for by the students, although some authorities make discretionary grants to help finance the courses. The degree courses cover a wide range (arts, mathematics, social sciences, science and technology) and are taken in a series of credit courses. Six credits have to be passed for an ordinary B.A. degree; eight for a degree at honours level.

The original idea was to have a university that would give working-class people who had missed out on advanced education a second chance. Although working-class people have enrolled, they are still very much in the minority. Teachers seeking a degree or a second degree have been its most usual students, while housewives and skilled and managerial workers have also been high up on the Open University lists.

A guide for applicants may be obtained from the Open University Admissions Office (addresses are listed in the Appendix).

Ordinary Level See O-level.

Ordinary National Certificate See ONC.

Ordinary National Diploma See OND.

Outward Bound Trust Based on the spartan but exhilarating methods used by the German educationist Kurt Hahn, the founder of Gordonstoun, the Trust runs residential courses lasting about twenty-six days each in several parts of the country for boys aged sixteen to nineteen and a half and girls aged sixteen to twenty. Special courses for juniors aged fourteen and a half to sixteen are also organized. The centres, which specialize in giving youngsters a sense of self-discipline and self-confidence through tough sports, adventure and physical fitness, are at Aberdovey (Wales), Burghead

(Morayshire), Ullswater (Lake District), Holne Park (Devon) and Towyn (Merioneth).

For full details and fees, contact address listed in Appendix.
See: Gordonstoun.

P

Parents Parents and parental choice have become one of the main subjects for discussion during the Great Debate which was opened in 1976 and continued through 1977. The role of the parent in education has been considered vital since the 1944 Education Act, but that role has often been seriously neglected. There are now a large number of organizations devoted to the parental role. The following, some of which are also dealt with in more detail elsewhere in this book, are among the main groups.

Confederation for the Advancement of State Education (CASE) An organization whose members are mostly interested parents devoted to the improvement of facilities and opportunities in all publicly-financed education.

Advisory Centre for Education (ACE) set up in 1960 to give parents the advice and information about schools and children's problems that they might be unable to obtain easily elsewhere.

Homes and School Council This produces a large variety of pamphlets specifically addressed to parents. It was set up by ACE, CASE and the National Confederation for Parent-Teacher Associations.

National Council for One-Parent Families (formerly the National Council for the Unmarried Mother and her Child) This provides practical help and moral support as well as numerous helpful publications for the single parents of more than one million children.

Gingerbread A pressure group concerned with the welfare and legal rights of one-parent families. It has about 130 branches throughout Britain.

Mothers in Action Another pressure group for one-parent families. It publishes a monthly bulletin called *Target*, covering child care, housing, employment and educational opportunities.

Parents' National Educational Union (PNEU) A body that assists parents who wish to educate their children at home.

For address to contact, see Appendix.

See: Advisory Centre for Education; CASE; Parents' National Educational Union; PTA.

Parents' Evenings The number of times the school is opened to parents depends largely on the school, but generally such evenings are held at least once a year, often once each term. It is an occasion for parents to meet their children's teachers and discuss progress and problems, see their children's work in the classroom and meet other parents. The way these occasions are run also depends largely on individual schools. Some teachers prefer to run an evening on an appointments system, giving each parent a rough idea of what time to come to the class. This often avoids parents' having to stand around in a queue, sometimes for anything up to two hours, to speak to a particular teacher. Too many schools still arrange such evenings on a first-come-first-served basis, which can be time-consuming for the parents. Possibly the greatest problem faced by teachers is to see the parents whose children really do create difficulties, for such parents rarely come to the school. Perhaps the best method of solving this problem was inaugurated by Dr Rhodes Boyson, the MP, when he was headmaster of Highbury Grove Comprehensive for Boys in Islington, North London. His school was divided into houses and each house held its own parents' evening. The housemaster, or a teacher delegated by him, would stand at the entrance with a register and tick each parent's name as he or she entered. The following day, the register was carefully studied and a letter, signed by the headmaster, would be sent to every parent who did *not* attend. It would regret this non-attendance, underline the importance of parents' evenings, explain that some teachers had looked forward to meeting the parents concerned and give the date of the next such evening. If they did not turn up then, they would be visited at home by a teacher or counsellor.

Parents' National Educational Union (PNEU) An organization founded in 1888 by Charlotte Mason (1842–1923), Victorian educationist who believed that parents could teach their children themselves in their own homes. There are now a number of Charlotte Mason schools in the private sector, which practise her theories. The PNEU provides parents with complete education courses for children from the age of three or four to eighteen. The parents act as teachers and are so treated by the organization, which supplies them with regular timetables, lessons and examinations. The latter are sent to the PNEU headquarters in London twice a year for marking. It is meant mainly for parents who live abroad or at long distances from any school. The PNEU will accept parents living in Britain only if they have thoroughly sound reasons for not sending their child or children to school and if they have had the approval of their local education authority.

For address to contact, see Appendix.

See: Home Teaching.

Parent-Teacher Associations, National Confederation of
A voluntary body with some 2,500 member associations representing the interests of more than 1,000,000 parents. It is represented on a number of bodies, including the Schools Council and the Council for Educational Advance. It also represents the United Kingdom on such bodies as the International Union of Family Organizations and the International Confederation of Parents. It holds an annual conference, helps parents and schools with advice, organizes debates, brains trusts, discussions, socials and outings to give parents and teachers the opportunity to meet more regularly and discuss problems about individual or groups of children.

For address to contact, see Appendix.

See: PTA.

Permanent Education This term has become better known in the original French – *éducation permanente* – and refers to the learning process that carries on long beyond school. We are always learning but should be given more opportunity to be educated continuously (at evening classes, further and higher education institutes for adults). The concept is an international one and joint research on the subject is being carried out by numerous international agencies (UNESCO, Council of Europe, etc.).

Further reading: *Permanent Education: A Compendium of Studies* (commissioned by the Council for Cultural Co-operation, Council of Europe, Strasbourg, 1970).

Personal Relationships This is an aspect of sex education dealing with the emotions and attitudes of schoolchildren towards their own and the opposite sex. The term may even be taken as a euphemism for sex education itself. In some schools it has created controversy and protests from parents because lessons have included delicate matters such as homosexuality, contraception and abortion.

See: Sex Education.

Physical Education Although the importance of physical education was fully recognized by the Ancient Greeks as a vital part of growing up, it was not until the late nineteenth century that 'drill' was introduced to British schools. But it was the 1944 Education Act which truly put PE on the academic map by insisting that local authorities were responsible not only for a child's mind but also his *body*. PE as it is now universally known has come a long way from the 'knees-bend-arms-stretch' days since 1944. Today it covers a multitude of activities, all designed to help a child grow strong and healthy. Rock climbing, swimming, dancing (music and movement), fencing, riding and sailing are now part of the PE curriculum (if schools have the money to spare on the necessary equipment). Gymnastics (on ropes, ladders and horses), judo, weight-lifting, the use of the trampoline, are all part of PE. Sport halls now carry some very sophisticated equipment indeed. Prior to 1944, PT (physical training) was often given in the school yard or playing field.

Physical Education Association Founded in 1899 as the Ling Physical Education Association to encourage the scientific study of Physical Education, Health Education and Recreation, it gives active help to the continuous improvement in this country and abroad of the physical health of the community.

For address to contact, see Appendix.

See: Physical Education.

Piaget, Jean (1896–) Swiss philosopher, teacher and psychologist. He has been professor of child psychology and history of scientific thought at the University of Geneva since 1929. His ideas that children believe the world to revolve around themselves and that night falls when they decide to go to sleep remain unquestioned in the world of educational psychology. The child, according to Piaget, will gradually discover his own little world through touch and smell and experience and continual play. If he is deprived of these important factors, his entire development could be retarded and seriously harmed. A child under the age of seven might imagine that a tall, thin bottle holds more water than a short, fat one, or that a tall person is older than a short person. More logical thought and rationalization begin from the age of seven, and it is virtually useless to discuss abstract ideas with children before that age. Language, numeracy, morality gradually develop as the child's powers of reasoning advance. Piaget has often been misunderstood with the result that the under-sevens have been left to 'discover for themselves' without any proper guidance from teachers.

Further reading: *The Developmental Psychology of Jean Piaget* by J. H. Flavell (Van Nostrand, New Jersey, 1963); *Psychology and Epistemology* by Jean Piaget and Barbel Inhelder (Penguin, 1972).

Pitman, Sir James (1901–) Inventor and proponent of ita – the initial teaching alphabet – which helps children to learn to read. He is the grandson of Sir Isaac Pitman, inventor of Pitman shorthand. He is also a committee member of the Simplified Spelling Society and among the trustees of the will of George Bernard Shaw entrusted to carry out Shaw's wish for the publication of the British alphabet.

See: Initial Teaching Alphabet.

Playgroups These are not schools and are not under the control of the Department of Education or the local authority, so they vary greatly. Generally, these groups take children aged from three to five for up to four hours a day, charging a reasonable fee. Most are run by voluntary groups, often with the help of mothers, but some are run by the local council and come under the auspices of the social services department. A council grant can be obtained for starting a playgroup. The service of such groups can be invaluable, for toddlers can learn a large variety of educational and social skills through play and by mixing with other children of their own age. The Pre-School Playgroups Association has been formed to encourage mothers to start playgroups and to help run them. It gives useful advice through its many local branches and publishes both a magazine, *Contact*, and a newspaper, *Playgroup News*, once a term.

For address to contact, see Appendix.

Further reading: *Playgroups in an Area of Social Need* by A. Joseph and J. Parfit, for the National Children's Bureau (National Foundation for Educational Research, 1972).

Plowden Report The report published in 1967 by the Central Advisory Council for Education, then under the chairmanship of Lady Plowden, as *Children and their Primary Schools*. The Council was asked in 1963 by Sir Edward (now Lord) Boyle, the then Minister of Education, to look at all aspects of primary education and the transition to secondary education. It made 197 recommendations, among which were: better contact between home and school; the designation of educational priority areas in which schools should be given preferential treatment through better resources and where teachers should be paid slightly better salaries than those in better-off areas; the setting up of community schools; the improved education of immigrants; a massive expansion of nursery education;

the admission of children to primary schools in the September following their fifth birthday. Generally, it is considered to be the classic blueprint for better primary education.

Further reading: *Children and their Primary Schools* (HMSO, two volumes, 1967); *Perspectives on Plowden*, edited by R. S. Peters (Routledge & Kegan Paul, 1969).

See: Community Schools; Educational Priority Area; Positive Discrimination.

Pocket Money A sum of money usually given weekly by parents to their children as spending money for their personal use. Amounts given differ and the question of how much a parent *should* give is a difficult one. Too much could spoil a child and cause resentment and jealousy among his friends. Too little, on the other hand, could create other complications in a commercially geared society. Children should be allowed to handle money, get to know its value and to appreciate the importance of saving (though inflation has tended to devalue savings rapidly, the principle still applies). By 1977 values, and purely as a rough guide, a weekly 20p to a ten-year-old should suffice, rising by 10, 15 or 20p a year (perhaps from the birthday or as a special reward for good work, helpfulness, etc.). Obviously, amounts depend entirely on the financial situation of the parents, but a well-off parent would be acting counter-productively to shower a child with easily-earned pound notes.

Politics in Education Although all teaching may be considered as indoctrination, party politics should be kept out of the classroom – by order of the local education authority. Teachers found to be preaching politics in such a way as to be indoctrinating their pupils along party political lines, can be suspended and, after careful investigation, dismissed. This does not mean that a teacher is not allowed to participate in political meetings, demonstrations, etc., outside school hours. He or she may belong to any political party or organization and even sell party journals in the street. The teacher's private life is, within reason, no concern of the local authority. However, once the teacher brings those political prejudices into the classroom, be they right or left-wing, it becomes the concern of that teacher's employers. Attempts in 1977 at the annual conference of the National Union of Teachers to ban from schools all teachers who are members of the extreme right-wing National Front failed. The rules of democracy are fairly straightforward in this field.

Parents whose children bring them evidence of political indoctrination by teachers *during lessons* may (and should) complain at once to the head teacher, the chairman of school managers/governors and the chief education officer of the local authority.

This does not mean that teachers are debarred from discussing all forms of politics in the classroom. It would be difficult to ignore, say, Marx or Hitler in modern history lessons, or to fail to put political labels on present or past prime ministers and other prominent politicians. Clear, but *objective* teaching of politics, particularly to senior pupils, is necessary and permissible.

Polytechnics Between 1969 and 1973, thirty groupings of well-established educational institutions in England and Wales were formally designated as polytechnics, following proposals contained in a White Paper published in 1966. Mostly based on former colleges of science and technology, together with colleges of art and commerce, the polytechnics provide both full-time and sandwich courses that span the arts, science and technology, art and design, business studies and education at postgraduate, undergraduate, diploma and certificate levels. Though concentrating mainly on vocational courses, they also provide high academic standards. Almost all degrees are validated by the Council for National Academic Awards and are of an equivalent standard to degrees offered by universities.

By 1976, about 100,000 students were enrolled on full-time and sandwich courses. Of these, about 65,000 were studying for first degrees and for higher qualifications. A further 120,000 students were on part-time or shorter, post-experience, vocational courses.

In April 1970, the directors of all thirty polytechnics established a Committee of Directors of Polytechnics, which is an advisory body concerning itself with all aspects of polytechnics and higher education. It gives evidence and expresses its composite views on such relevant matters to inquiries and Government bodies.

For address to contact, see Appendix.

Further reading: *The New Polytechnics* by E. Robinson (Cornmarket Press, 1968); *Polytechnic Courses Handbook*, annual directory of courses, published by the Committee of Directors of Polytechnics.

See: Council for National Academic Awards (CNAA); Sandwich Courses.

Positive Discrimination Discrimination in favour of those believed to be socially deprived – e.g. immigrants, the poor living in dilapidated housing, served by old, poorly equipped schools. Generally, this is the policy in areas designated as educational priority areas where greater resources are granted to schools than to those schools in socially advantaged areas.

See: Educational Priority Area; Plowden Report.

Prefects Originally the title given to responsible persons charged with the administration or keeping of law and order in ancient Rome, and still thus used in France for chief administrative officers in the départements of the country, the term was applied to senior pupils in schools throughout Britain who kept discipline among the younger children. They were believed first to have been appointed in about 1270 at Merton College in order to 'herd' pupils to Chapel. Later, they helped out teachers in schools with insufficient staff and gradually took on the role of disciplinarians, a kind of internal police force to keep the younger pupils in their place. The heads of public schools came to depend on prefects more and more to help in the regimentation of pupils and their chastisement.

Normally, prefects were appointed by heads and housemasters for their seniority and responsibility. It became an honour to be a prefect and brought certain advantages to the holders of the post. Grammar schools were quick to recognize the advantages of such a force of (normally) sixth formers who would maintain law and order within the school and even outside it by making sure that pupils were properly dressed, behaved decently and kept school rules. They acted as playground patrols, supervised classes when teachers were absent, even helped younger pupils with their academic work and often organized extra-mural activities such as sporting fixtures and societies.

At many public schools, prefects held so high a status that they not only had the right to administer corporal punishment (and often did) but had certain perks, such as a common room of their own and the power to appoint younger boys (usually first formers) to act as their 'fags' – cleaning their shoes, making their tea and running errands for them.

A recent survey carried out by David Reynolds, a lecturer in social administration at University College, Cardiff, showed that big comprehensive schools which have retained the tradition of a prefectoral system suffer less indiscipline than those without prefects. It helped the more senior pupils to become 'leaders' and appreciate the high responsibility bestowed upon them. The survey is fully reported in *The Process of Schooling*, one of the Sociological Readers used by the Open University in its Schooling and Society course.

See: Monitor; Fagging.

Prep An abbreviation for preparation, that is, work done individually in preparation for or revision of lessons given in various subjects.

The term is almost exclusively applied to schools in the independent sector, particularly boarding schools, where children will be set specific work to do in after-school hours. In the state school sector, the more usual term for this activity is homework.

See: Homework.

Preparatory Schools Independent schools which prepare pupils for the common entrance examination to admit them to public schools. The preparatory school, or 'prep' school, takes pupils usually from the age of eight up to the age of thirteen, although some keep pupils up to the age of fifteen (the average age of entry to public schools is thirteen years six months). There are more than 450 preparatory schools for boys and about 100 for girls in Britain, all recognized as efficient by the Department of Education and Science.

Further reading: *The Public and Preparatory Schools Year Book* and *The Girls' School Year Book*, both published annually by A. & C. Black, which give details, including fees, names of heads and staff and curricula of all recognized preparatory schools.

See: Incorporated Association of Preparatory Schools.

Primary School A school which covers the education of a child from the age of five (the compulsory school starting age) to eleven-plus (when the child enters a secondary school). The first level of the school is the infant school (for children aged from five to seven), where the child should be taught reading, writing and arithmetic. The second level is the junior school when these basic subjects should be perfected and advanced with other subjects, such as history, geography and even a second language.

In future, with the birth rate in decline, a number of primary schools will face the threat of closure. Others are likely to have to turn their classes into nursery classes (for children aged from three to five). Some primary schools now take children only to the age of eight or nine, the children transferring at that age to a middle school until the age of thirteen or fourteen, when they proceed to the final stage of compulsory education.

See: Infant School; Junior School; Middle School.

Probationary Teacher The first year of a teacher's service after qualification is a probationary period, during which he or she must satisfy the Secretary of State of his or her practical ability to teach. The local authority has been delegated to check whether this requirement has been met and may either recommend the teacher for fully-qualified status or for an extra period of six months in probation.

Many schools tend to give the probationer a somewhat lighter timetable than the experienced staff. There is usually also a more experienced teacher who acts as general friend and guide to the probationer.

See: Qualified Teacher; Teacher Training.

Professional Association of Teachers A union established in 1970 following a series of strikes by teachers in other unions. Members are pledged never to go on strike, believing that 'teaching is a profession with responsibility to the community', and have been pressing for the setting up of a General Teachers' Council, similar in aims to the General Medical Council, with a code of conduct. The PAT caught on quickly. With an initial recruitment of 300 teachers, most of them never having belonged to a union previously but with others who resigned from more militant unions in protest against strikes, it now claims more than 10,000 members. Student membership is free; probationary teachers are also free for first term of service and there is a nominal subscription for the first two years of teaching.

For address to contact, see Appendix.

PTA (Parent-Teacher Associations) There has not yet been any legal support for such organizations which form a link between parents and teachers at any particular school. Although there is nothing to stop parents from joining together to form a parents' association, they must first obtain the agreement of the head teacher for the formation of a parent-teacher association. There are still many heads who oppose such groups and regard them with suspicion as a possible interference in the running of the school. Generally, PTAs tend to be a help rather than a hindrance. For advice on how to set up a PTA, consult the National Confederation of Parent-Teacher Associations.

Further reading: *Children and their Primary Schools* – Plowden Report (HMSO, 1967); *Parent-Teacher Relations in Primary Schools* (Department of Education and Science, HMSO, 1968); *School and Home* by E. Goodacre (National Foundation for Educational Research).

See: Parent-Teacher Associations, National Confederation of.

Public Schools Independent, fee-paying schools, many of which have boarding provision and admit pupils aged from thirteen to eighteen-plus. There are more than 1200 private schools, of which some 200 can be described as the 'top public schools' (those participating in the Headmasters' Conference). It has always mystified foreigners (and many an Englishman) why a private school should be called 'public'. The explanation goes back to the Middle Ages when the first grammar schools made their appearance. Mainly based on the Christianity of St Paul or the stoicism of Plato, they quickly attracted boys (girls' schools were unheard of until the nineteenth century) from all over the country. Thus, instead of being schools for the local child populace, they broadened their scope and intakes to a wider public – hence, public schools.

Although only a small percentage (about five per cent of the secondary school age group) go to independent schools, the public schools' share of the university intake of undergraduates exceeds twenty per cent. Public schools have been seen by egalitarians as bastions of élitism and privilege that should be abolished. A Public Schools Commission set up in 1966 sought to integrate these schools into the maintained sector. The phasing out of direct grant schools, which form part of the public school system began in September 1976. The result was that most of them decided to go fully independent.

See: Direct Grant School; Donnison Report; Headmasters' Conference; Newsom Reports.

Public Schools Bursars' Association (PSBA) An organization for bursars of public schools, giving advice on all administrative matters, including salaries of administrative staff, income tax, charitable status, etc. It issues regular bulletins and pamphlets containing such advice.

For address to contact, see Appendix.

Punishment Punishment in schools can range from detention after school hours, the withdrawal of certain privileges (keeping in class during breaks, banning from taking part in sporting activities), imposition of extra work or lines, to corporal punishment. Particularly serious offences can lead to more severe punishment, such as suspension or expulsion.

Further reading: *Discipline in Schools*, edited by L. Stenhouse (Pergamon Press, 1967); *Discipline in Schools*, edited by B. Turner (Ward Lock, 1973); *A Survey of Rewards and Punishments in Schools* by M. E. Highfield and A. Pinsent, National Foundation for Educational Research (Newnes, 1952).

See: Corporal Punishment; Sanctions.

Punishment Book A book kept in the school office or in the head's study in which all executions of corporal punishment are recorded. It has to list the name of the pupil so punished, the date of punishment, by whom it was ordered, by whom it was inflicted (normally the head or a deputy), by what method (cane, slipper), where it was inflicted, how many strokes were given and the reason for the punishment. It exists as a protection for the teacher in question against any possible allegations of unjust or sadistic assault. Although all inflictions of corporal punishment *should* be entered in the book, it is believed that only a small proportion of them are.

Further reading: *A Last Resort? – Corporal Punishment in Schools*, edited by P. Newell (Penguin Education, 1972); *Teachers and the Law* by G. R. Barrell (Methuen, 1966).

See: Corporal Punishment.

Pupil Power Following the student unrest of the late sixties, school pupils began to seek rights of their own and demonstrated for an end to corporal punishment, the abolition of school uniforms, better sex education (including lessons on homosexuality as well as heterosexuality) and full participatory rights in the running of schools. Strikes were organized and a national body, called the Schools Action Union, was set up. This has now almost disappeared but has been replaced by a more streamlined, better run organization called the National Union of School Students, which is advised and assisted by the National Union of Students. Pupils have been successful in numerous areas, and scores of secondary schools now have pupil governors sitting on their boards. Whether such representation is legal or not is open to question. The Department of Education, when informed by the Greater Manchester borough of Tameside in 1977 that it wanted to increase the number of pupil governors on its twenty-two secondary schools from one to two, replied that it was 'illegal', since minors (under age eighteen) had no rights as trustees. There is, however, no statute to back this pronouncement, and the Taylor Report on school government (September 1977) proposed that pupils should be included on governing boards.

See: Students, National Union of School (NUSS); Taylor Report.

Q

Quaker Schools Nine schools, mostly boarding, are run by the Society of Friends, with about three thousand pupils aged from thirteen to eighteen. The first of these was founded in 1702. Details of fees, scholarships and bursaries may be found in the publication *Friends' Schools*, while the Society also publishes a pamphlet *Quakers and their Schools*, which sets out the Quaker philosophy of education.

For address to contact, see Appendix.

Qualified Teacher All teachers in the maintained sector of education have to be qualified before they are allowed to teach. This is achieved by passing a three-year course at a college of education or, in the case of a university graduate, a one-year teacher training course, after which a one-year period of probation must be successfully completed inside a school. The fully-qualified rule for primary school teachers and graduates was introduced in 1970 following a lengthy campaign by teachers' unions. Before 1970, there were some 8000 non-qualified teachers and 16,000 untrained graduates in a total teaching force of about 300,000. The present force of some 431,000 contains only teachers of fully qualified status, although it includes perhaps a handful who have been given a special dispensation because of their outstanding contribution to the teaching profession, although without qualifications, over a long period of years.

See: Probationary Teacher; Teacher Training.

Quinquennium A period spanning five years. The word often describes the five-year period spanned by the grants made to universities by the University Grants Committee to cover their recurrent expenditure. Universities used to work out their finances, including plans for new buildings, equipment, etc., on this five-year period. However, the recent inflationary spiral has forced them to work on a hand-to-mouth basis, applying for and receiving grants annually.

See: University Grants Committee.

Quota System The method of seeing that each local authority has sufficient teachers to man its schools. In a sense, it is a system of rationing teachers to authorities so that those in deprived areas should not be short of the necessary teachers in their schools. Quotas are recommended in circulars sent to authorities by the Department of Education and Science. They are not legally binding documents but authorities are generally advised to keep as near to their quotas as possible. Originally devised when there was a serious shortage of teachers in order to ensure that newly-qualified teachers were evenly distributed, the system has been less appropriate in recent years when teachers were in ample supply, particularly in the late seventies when, because of miscalculations in the projected birth rates, there was a rapid rise in the unemployment of teachers.

R

Rate Support Grant (RSG) By far the most important sources of finance for education come from local rates and income tax. Local authorities do the actual spending of money in real terms on schools, books, equipment, colleges, teachers, etc. The Government (not via the Department of Education but via the Department of the Environment) contributes a block allocation of money to the local authorities to spend on all types of services, including hospitals, roads, housing and the like. Education is just one of those services, albeit the biggest, with something in the region of eighty-five per cent of the total resources spent on it. Of this eighty-five per cent, about sixty-five per cent comes from the Government and it is this element that is called the rate support grant. The Department of Education can only use its influence on local authorities' spending on the education sector. It cannot dictate how much should be spent. Authorities submit their annual estimates of how much they are expecting to spend on each service in the following year(s) and the amounts are then negotiated between the various local authority bodies and the Government.

Further reading: *A Guide to English Schools* by T. Burgess (Penguin, 1969).

See: DES; Local Education Authorities.

Reading This is probably the most controversial of the basic subjects a child must learn. At what age should a child start to learn to read? Should parents teach the child to read before he starts school? These are just two of the many questions posed in the long debate on literacy. Although it has generally been felt that no child could – or even should – start to read before the age of five, one child in every four now starts school able to read after a fashion. Many children are able to recognize and read letters of the alphabet by the time they are one year old; others can still not read by the time they are eight. The subject has to be tackled with great care and wisdom.

Parents should read as much and as often as possible to their young children. But the parent should not force a child to read, teaching it letters and words from books, unless the child expresses a desire for reading and enjoys the exercise. Parents would be well advised to visit their local infant school (to which they will be sending their child) to find out which of the many different reading methods is being taught there. This will avoid the child's becoming confused later on when he actually goes to that school.

The view that a child will read when he is ready to do so often holds good, though some teachers take this recipe too literally. A child who cannot read by the time he is eight requires immediate remedial help.

A child who finds exceptional difficulty in learning the sounds of letters *might* be hard of hearing; if he cannot form collections of letters into the word they represent, he *might* be dyslexic. There are numerous tests that could determine whether the child's difficulties can be traced to some physical handicap or even a mental one. The handbook which goes with the *Ladybird* reading scheme, gives nineteen preconditions to reading, of which the most important are: Can the child hear and see properly? Is he free from speech defect? Is his general health satisfactory? Does he appear to be seriously retarded in intelligence? Does he ask questions about the objects and happenings in his environment? Does he understand and carry out oral instructions? Does he listen satisfactorily to a story? (No doubt, it would depend on what the story is and how well or badly it is being told before one can decide whether the child's interest is being held.) Can he re-tell a simple story in fairly logical sequence? Can he see similarities and differences in simple drawings? Is he generally self-reliant, not continually asking for help, and able to work on his own for short periods? Can he match word with word? And – possibly the most important – does he show signs of wanting to read?

In general, teachers should be allowed to *teach* children to read and parents should *encourage* their children to read. Certainly, parents should listen to children reading aloud and help them with any difficult words. Parents ought to be allowed into primary schools to help teachers by hearing children read (some, but by no means all, such schools have already opened their doors to parents). But parents should not take teachers too literally when they are told: 'On no account must you interfere in the learning process.' If matters were left to some teachers, parents would not even allow their children to come into contact with words and would throw all books out of the window. Such attitudes are little short of disgraceful. But there are also some parents who go too far and who force their children to read, long before they are ready, books they do not like. This attitude goes to the other extreme and is likely to put children off books and reading for life.

Further reading: *Give Your Child a Chance* by B. Kemble (W. H. Allen, 1970); *Perception and Understanding in Young Children* by P. Bryant (Methuen, 1974); *Reading and the Dyslexic Child* by R. M. N. Crosby (Souvenir Press, 1968); *Early Reading and Writing* by R. Minovi (George Allen & Unwin, 1976); *Reading and Writing before School* by F. Hughes (Jonathan Cape, 1971); *A Language for Life* – the Bullock Report (HMSO, 1975).

See: Dyslexia; Illiteracy; Initial Teaching Alphabet.

Regulations The Secretary of State for Education and Science has powers under the 1944 Education Act to issue regulations to all local education authorities. These are statutory rules and have the power of the law. In them, he or she is able to instruct authorities of Government policies and demands, covering a large number of matters from the length of the school day to what building materials should (or should not) be used. Such regulations must be complied with. However, they often offer authorities (and the Government) a let-out clause. For example, in 1959, regulations laid down the maximum number of children per class – forty for a primary school, thirty for a secondary school class. Although thirty children per class in either school has long been the policy of the teaching unions, many schools still exceed this number. Local authorities argue that the let-out clause gave them this right. It stated that the maximum number was laid down 'provided that, if owing to the shortage of teachers or other unavoidable circumstances, it is not possible to comply with this regulation, the number of pupils . . . shall be such as is reasonable in all the circumstances.'

See: Circulars.

Religious Education (RE) Under the Education Act of 1944, the teaching of religion together with a daily assembly for an act of worship became compulsory in all state schools, although parents have the right to withdraw their children from such classes or assemblies. In voluntary aided schools RE falls under the control of boards of managers or governors. There are growing factions, particularly the humanists, who wish to have the subject removed from the syllabus.

See: Agreed Syllabus; Assembly.

Remedial Classes These are generally considered to be short-term classes for children who are backward in one or more subjects. A child who is, say, retarded in one of the basic subjects (reading, writing or arithmetic) is given special teaching help in a class attended by a small number of pupils under a specialist teacher. Many schools, particularly secondary schools of the comprehensive variety, have remedial teachers on their staff rolls. Some remedial lessons take place in child guidance clinics or special centres. Children who are extremely backward educationally may be designated as educationally subnormal (ESN) and sent to special schools.

Further reading: *The Slow Learner* by M. F. Cleugh (Methuen, 1968).

See: Educationally Subnormal; Slow Learners; Special Education.

Remuneration of Teachers Acts Two such Acts were passed, one in 1963 and another in 1965. The first came about after the then Minister of Education refused to accept salary scales proposed for teachers. He had wanted to increase the differentials between scales, but the Burnham Committee was adamant. A special Act was then passed so that the new scales could be paid in accordance with what the Minister wanted. Two years later, the Remuneration of Teachers Act (1965) repealed the first and added to the Burnham Committees a representative for the Secretary of State for Education and Sciences. It also provided for the setting up of an independent arbitration body to resolve any deadlock on the committees and for the retrospective payment of salary awards.

See: Arbitration; Burnham Committees.

Reorganization Originally this meant the changeover from elementary schools to primary and secondary schools – i.e. those children aged from five to eleven were placed in primary schools, while those aged eleven-plus were placed into secondary schools where they remained until the statutory leaving age. This reorganization was proposed by the 1926 report *Education of the Adolescent*, which became better known as the Hadow Report. Today, the term refers to yet another radical change in educational structure – the change from the selective secondary schools system to non-selective, all-ability comprehensive schools and the tributary changes involved, such as the setting up of middle schools that take pupils from primary schools at the age of eight or nine and keep them up to the age of twelve or thirteen before sending them on to the senior schools.

See: Comprehensive Education; Middle School.

Residual Income The income which remains after various allowable deductions have been made from the gross sum. Such deductions include mortgage interest payments, other dependants in the family (children, dependant in-laws or relations living in the same house and having to be financially supported), superannuation and union membership subscriptions.

The residual income is used in the 'means test' to calculate the amount a student should or might receive as a grant (see Student Grants). It is the student's parent who is thus means-tested. Students are also means-tested; their grants are reduced if any personal income exceeds £215. In 1976, it was assumed that, on average, a gross income of £3300 would produce a residual income of about £2700. The latter figure was then regarded as the threshold below which parents were required to pay nothing towards the grant. But from £2700, the parent was expected to contribute £30 towards grants, rising by £20 for every £100 of additional residual income up to £4200 and £10 for every £100 thereafter.

The threshold was raised from September 1977 and parents with residual incomes of £3200 were expected to contribute only £20 towards grants with initial rises of £20 for every £100 of residual income.

Thus, if a student at, say a provincial university (maximum grant: £1010 a year) had a parent whose residual income was £4000, the parent would be required to pay £180 towards the son's or daughter's grant, while the local authority would pay the student £1010 minus £180 = £830.

Many students complain that their parents fail to give them their contributions and some students, particularly those whose grants comprise only the minimum £80 or slightly more, suffer real hardship. The law cannot force parents to pay. This is a matter between them and the students concerned.

Scales for parental contributions and residual incomes are now revised annually along with grants (around March–May). For up-to-date information, inquiries should be made to the National Union of Students (NUS) or the Department of Education and Science (Student Awards Branch, DES).

See: Student Grants, Student Fees.

Rising Fives Children who are allowed to start school full-time before the statutory attendance age of five in that they may be given a place at the start of the term in which their fifth birthday falls. With the drop in the birth rate, more such places are now being found for the rising five-year-old, but the law still only requires a local education authority to provide a school place for a child at the beginning of the term *after* the fifth birthday has been reached.

Robbins Report This major report on higher education, published in 1963 under the chairmanship of Lord Robbins, called for the rapid expansion of universities and polytechnics to cope with the fast-growing demand from school leavers for higher education. It recommended that places should be made available for 390,000 students in full-time higher education by 1973-4 and for 560,000 in 1980-1. It foresaw a crisis in education if these demands were not met. It also recommended that colleges of advanced technology be given the status of university in order to help meet the greater demand and that six new universities be set up close to big industrial centres. The report wanted to see closer collaboration between the Government, industry and higher education. As it turned out, expansion was slower than expected, mainly because of inflation, growing unemployment and the cuts in educational expenditure that were to become such important issues in the seventies. The report also led to the establishment of the Council for National Academic Awards (CNAA).

See: Council for National Academic Awards; Universities.

ROSLA Raising of the school leaving age.

See: School Leaving Age.

Rousseau, Jean Jacques (1712-78) French philosopher whose books included two treatises, *La Nouvelle Héloïse* published in 1761, and *Emile* one year later, which had a lasting effect on major educational reforms. He believed that the child, if left virtually alone, would be able to discover knowledge – that is, all he needed to know – by himself and that the interference of adult teachers often hampered rather than helped the child. He wanted children to learn by touch, and to experience learning from natural surroundings. This was pure romanticism and appealed to the instigators of the Revolution that was to overthrow the *ancien régime* in France in 1789.

Like many other educational theories, Rousseau's have been misunderstood and misinterpreted. His Emile had to be guided along the path of discovery. Some teachers, however, feel that the child should be left entirely to his own devices – so much so that the learning of a poem by heart is almost considered 'wicked'.

Rules Schools, like clubs, must have rules for their members. What these rules are and how many of them are listed is left to individual schools (or clubs). Some schools will insist on the wearing of uniforms but even here the rules differ, since certain schools will stipulate expensive blazers, hats, capes, socks and ties while others will keep to a more simple (and relatively cheap) uniform of the kind obtainable from almost any department store. Breach of the uniform rule (e.g. girls' wearing trousers instead of neat grey skirts) can lead to instant suspension.

But rules apply to teachers as well as taught. To illustrate this, there follows a quotation from the rules of one big comprehensive school in the London borough of Enfield. 'Our basic outlook is that the teacher, not the children, is in control of the classroom,' says the headmaster's rule sheet for teachers. 'To be in control, you need to attend to each of the following:

'Do not accept rudeness or disobedience. In order to maintain this rule, the teacher should: a) quietly but firmly rebuke failure to come up to standards required in courtesy and conduct. Repetition is punishable by detention either at dinner time or after 3.30 p.m. or both, during which time extra work should be set; b) discuss troublesome pupils with form tutor, head of subject or year, deputy head or head; c) do not send disobedient pupils out of the room while the lesson continues, but this can be done if you ensure that the rest of the class has work to do, while you then go outside to have a quiet word with the pupil concerned. You may then re-admit the child who is likely to settle down to work.

'Normally, you should not hit or assault a pupil or grasp him or her. Corporal punishment should not be used. If a pupil is assaulting another person, appropriate action should be taken immediately and this may well include firmly grasping the assailant and pulling him or her firmly away.

'Between rooms, in the hall, in corridors, and in the playground or on the field, do not walk past indiscipline. Question any child who walks by you during lesson time. He should be in someone's lesson or undertaking private study, so do not hesitate to take appropriate action if you suspect deception or truancy.

'Do not permit a class without a teacher to be noisy or not working.

'Do not permit dangerous play at breaktimes. Look out for bullying and deal with it.

'Organize your room and routine: pupils will need to be taught *your* ways of doing things, so it is helpful if you work out definite ideas. (These include such items as distributing books and equipment at the beginning of each lesson; collecting them back at the end; inspecting pupils' appearance as a routine at the start and end of lessons.)

'In the case of vandalism, culprits, if identifiable, must be dealt with immediately, by reporting to the head of upper or lower school. Where culprits are not identifiable, an immediate investigation must be launched, such inquiry to take precedence over other school activities.'

This school includes rules for parents. It provides pupils with a homework diary in which all homework set must be entered. Parents must sign the diary weekly and enter comments as to what they think of the homework, their children's capabilities in doing it and if they considered it sufficient. This method helps to involve parents and offers them a chance to co-operate with the school.

At another school, a more progressive one in the Hampstead area, children are forbidden to climb on roofs of buildings, or damage any school property. They are not allowed to introduce skate-boards or any other equipment that would endanger pupils or others; they may not leave school unless they are fifth formers or senior; a nearby hospital's premises are out of bounds. Bubble gum and other offensive types of confectionery are not permitted during lessons. Teachers are forbidden to use corporal punishment, nor must they make children write lines, since these are considered a waste of time.

Most schools will punish breaches of rules. Depending on the severity of the offence, such punishment can range from detentions to suspensions.

See: Sanctions.

S

Salaries See Burnham Committees.

Sanctions Types of punishment for the constantly ill-disciplined pupil or constant disrupter of classes vary. The most usual include:

  Corporal Punishment See separate article.

  Detention See separate article.

Expulsion See separate article.

Lines This rather outmoded punishment, whereby a naughty pupil is given 100 or 1000 lines to write (I must not talk in class, etc.), rarely has the desired effect. Additional homework or picking up litter from the playground is usually more productive.

Report For the chronic offender, a report card is issued which has to be signed at the end of each lesson by the teacher concerned, with a brief account of the pupil's behaviour. A senior teacher must check this card at the end of the day before allowing the pupil to leave. If no improvement is shown after a given time, parents should be called to the school for discussion.

Separation Sending a disruptive pupil to a special unit within a school or just outside the main building for a period of time. If given plenty of work and close supervision, the pupil often mends his ways comparatively rapidly, especially as he no longer has an audience to whom to play.

Suspension See separate article.

Sandwich Courses Full-time courses for degrees or diplomas at colleges of further or higher education which are 'sandwiched' in such a way that students alternate periods of six months or more at college and in industry. Thus, a student would receive both theoretical training and practical training. Those students who are paid a salary throughout the period both of study and work in industry are said to be industry-based, while those in receipt of local authority grants would be college-based. This system, too, can be sandwiched in the sense that a college-based student would have to be found work within industry, during which time he would be paid a wage or salary just as other workers. The industry-based student might be paid only during his practical work training and go over to a local authority grant when he is at college.

SAU See Schools Action Union.

SCE See Education in Scotland (Examinations).

Scholarship An award of money from private or public funds, usually made following a competitive examination, which will give the holder of the award either a free education or a reduction in the fees of a university, college or public school. Some are 'closed scholarships' – that is, awards given, usually from a trust fund, to certain named groups of people, such as the sons/daughters of clergymen or certain businessmen or those living in a particular area of the country; others are 'open scholarships' – that is, they are available to anyone who applies for the examination.

The term was also applied to the eleven-plus examination which selected children for grammar schools.

Schonell, Sir Fred (1900–68) Australian educationist, Vice-Chancellor of the University of Queensland from 1960 until his death. He was previously professor of education at Queensland and at the universities of Swansea and Birmingham and from 1931 until the early war years, lecturer in educational psychology, Goldsmiths' College, London. He was best known for diagnosis and treatment of backward children and the *Schonell Reading Tests*, still widely used to grade reading norms of children aged from five upwards.

School Building What building programmes a local authority undertakes must first receive the blessing of the Secretary of State for Education, although the Department of Education does not pay for the building to be done. The local authority submits its plans two years in advance, estimating the amount of money it will need to spend. The Government, which has control over overall public expenditure, will either approve or reject the proposals. If it approves them, the local authority then has to find the money from loans financed by the rate support grant and the rates themselves. Two divisions of school building allocations exist, those for minor works and those for major works. The former allocation is for improvements or modest extensions to existing schools, while the latter is for the building of new schools.

Further reading: *A Guide to English Schools* by T. Burgess (Penguin, 1969).

See: Rate Support Grant.

School Certificate School leaving examination taken by pupils between the end of World War I and 1951. Unlike the present O-levels taken in the General Certificate of Education, the certificate involved sitting a set of compulsory examinations within a group of subjects. Unless English language and mathematics were passed, the entire Certificate examination had to be re-sat. At least five subjects had to be passed by candidates before a certificate was awarded. The SC was replaced in 1951 by the General Certificate of Education (Ordinary and Advanced levels), which could be taken subject by subject, thus allowing candidates to distinguish themselves in at least one field.

See: High School Certificate; Examinations.

School Government After two years of deliberations and innumerable 'leaks' in the Press, the Taylor Committee (chairman: Tom Taylor of Blackburn) finally published its long-awaited report in September 1977. Its radical proposals would produce wide-reaching changes in the government of schools. Briefly, these are as follows:

Each school is to have its own board of governors with equal representation being given to parents, teachers and representatives of the local community and the local education authority. The head teacher should always be a member of the board. Pupils should also be represented. (Although a number of authorities have already allowed pupil representation, an official change of this kind would require legislation. An official decree from the Department of Education advised Tameside Authority in 1977 that pupils could not be appointed or elected to boards as voting members as they were 'minors' and could, therefore, not hold public office of responsibility. However, there was no actual law pointing to such a direction.)

Elections would be held in every school for parent and pupil-governors: one quarter of each governing body should represent the local authority; one quarter should represent teachers and ancillary staff, automatically including the head; one quarter should be elected by all parents of children at the school including, in appropriate cases, pupils elected by their fellows. The remaining quarter should be co-opted by the other three groups from the local community.

The Governing Board should: 1. establish the school's objectives; 2. draw up the structure of learning and rules for the school; 3. have access in its task to the professional guidance of inspectors and advisers. Local authorities should run training courses for governors. No child should be debarred from the school (other than on medical grounds) except in accordance with procedures established by the local authority; no child should be expelled except by decision of the local authority.

See: Governors and Managers, Board of.

School Leaving Age Before the 1870 Education Act, children were able to leave school at the age of twelve, although there was no rigorous obligation to attend school and many children of younger years were already working. The 1870 Act raised the leaving age to thirteen and this became statutory ten years later. The Fisher Act of 1918 compelled children to stay on at school until the age of fourteen and so it remained until the 1944 Butler Act which made the leaving age fifteen (however, this was not implemented until 1947). The same Act also recommended that the age should be raised to sixteen as soon as possible. This was to have been implemented in 1970, but the Government in 1968 postponed the plan due to economic pressures.

Mrs Thatcher, Education Secretary in the Government of 1970, declared that the age would be raised to sixteen and this measure was implemented from 1 September 1972.

Boys and girls whose sixteenth birthdays fall between 1 September and 31 January may leave school at Easter; those with birthdays between 1 February and 31 August may leave from the Spring Bank Holiday in May, depending on what examination commitments they have.

School Meals Meals have to be provided by local authorities for pupils at schools (milk up to the age of seven is provided free). More than 6,000,000 meals are served each day during the school year (i.e. about 200 days) at a gross annual cost (1975–6 prices) of £471,000,000. The price of a meal up to September 1977 was 15p, after which it was increased to 25p. From the 15p charge, including special rates for adults taking meals at school, an income of £143,000,000 was recorded, leaving a net expenditure of £328,000,000. Meals are eaten by 5,640,000 pupils and 564,500 adults daily. Of pupils, 1,500,000 receive free meals; of the adults (teachers, supervisors, kitchen staff and others) fewer than 33,000 pay for meals. According to an analysis carried out in November 1976, the actual food element in the meal cost 16p, while 28p went on the cost of kitchen staff, clerical and administrative work, and 5p on running costs (fuel, transport, rent, rates, maintenance). There is a growing campaign, mainly among teachers, to have meals scrapped from the education budget.

School Phobia A chronic and very real fear of school, as opposed to intermittent dislike of attending school. It can sometimes be traced to a child's early traumatic experiences at kindergarten (nursery school) and it often requires psychological or even psychiatric treatment. Symptoms include habitual truanting and avoiding school as often as possible through a series of psychosomatic illnesses that may involve not only the usual head and stomach aches but also diarrhoea and vomiting.

School Population There are approximately 10,500,000 pupils aged five to eighteen in nearly 29,000 primary, 6,600 secondary and 1,800 special schools in the United Kingdom (i.e. England, Wales, Scotland and Northern Ireland).

School Records Confidential records are kept on all pupils and stored in school files. They have become a cause for concern among parents and some of the more radical bodies, simply because pupils and parents are not given access to the information contained in them. It is true that some teachers tend to write detrimental reports about pupils they simply do not like, but in general, these records are factual reports about a child's academic progress. They should note his abilities and weaknesses and, where relevant, any family background problems which could account for weaknesses or disciplinary shortcomings in the pupil. Clearly, such records, if well kept, can be invaluable to teachers, particularly in schools with big teacher turnovers or if the child is transferred from one school to another. They should not be regarded as 'criminal records' but should be amended regularly (where a child has 'turned over a new leaf') and destroyed once the child has left his last school. They should not (but sometimes are) be sent to future employers, although references may be based on the information contained in the cards.

Schools Establishments in which children are taught. They are divided into numerous categories: nursery, for children aged from three to five (although some take in children from the age of two); primary, for those aged five to eleven-plus — this category is subdivided into infant (age five to seven-plus) and junior (age seven-plus to eleven-plus); secondary, for those aged eleven-plus to eighteen-plus. The latter is subdivided into secondary modern, grammar and technical, although with reorganization in many areas of the country this system has been amalgamated into the all-ability, non-selective comprehensive.

Also within the state-maintained sector, there are special schools for the physically and mentally handicapped, for the deaf and blind or partially sighted and for the educationally subnormal (ESN). There are also hospital schools, operated within hospitals to give special tuition for children who are long-serving patients.

In the private sector, the above categories of children are also catered for in preparatory, direct grant and public schools.

See: Comprehensive Education; Direct Grant Schools; Grammar Schools; Infant School; Junior School; Nursery School; Preparatory Schools; Primary School; Public Schools; Special Schools; Tripartite System; Voluntary Schools.

Schools Action Union (SAU) A radical movement composed of pupils who campaign against the wearing of school uniforms, corporal punishment and the 'autocracy' of the head teacher. It blows hot and cold and has virtually disappeared except in small pockets, since it was largely superseded by the National Union of School

Students (NUSS). In the early seventies, when it was formed, it organized 'strikes' and demonstrations, with groups of pupils walking out of schools to march to local education offices to make their various demands. It is largely a publicity-seeking group under the leadership of left-wing extremists.

See: National Union of School Students.

Schools Council Its full name is the Schools Council for Curriculum and Examinations. It is the body, at present composed mainly of representatives of the teaching associations and unions, which formulates the curricula for both primary and secondary schools. Set up in 1964 by the Government, it is supported by funds from local authorities and central Government, and has so far spent in excess of £10 million on the development of school curricula and changes in the examinations system. It has its own staff and a governing council of seventy-six members who represent the wide spectrum of education.

The National Union of Teachers, biggest of the teacher associations, has seventeen members on this council. Others are (with members, hence voting figures, in brackets): National Association of Schoolmasters/Union of Women Teachers (4); National Association of Head Teachers (3); National Association of Teachers in Further and Higher Education (5); Committee of Vice-Chancellors and Principals (4); Headmasters' Association (2); Association of Headmistresses (2); Assistant Masters' Association (3); Association of Assistant Mistresses (3); Association of Principals of Colleges (2); University Council for the Education of Teachers (3); Technicians' Education Council (1); Council for National Academic Awards (1); National Foundation for Educational Research (1); all General Certificate of Education examining boards (1); all Certificate of Secondary Education examining boards (1); Inspectors and Advisers (1); Association of University Teachers (1); Trades Union Congress (1); Confederation of British Industry (1); Parent-Teacher Associations (1); Headmasters' Conference (1); Incorporated Association of Preparatory Schools (1); Association of County Councils (2); Association of Metropolitan Authorities (2); Association of Education Committees (2); Inner London Education Authority (1); Welsh Joint Education Committee (2); Society of Education Officers (1); Church of England Board of Education Schools Council (1); Catholic Education Council (1); Free Church Federal Council (1); Department of Education and Science (3). Not more than ten others may be co-opted by the governing council.

The Council has been severely criticized from a number of quarters for being top-heavy on teacher representation. There are now moves to bring more parents, employers and other lay persons with an interest in education and the reforms of curricula and examinations on to the governing council and the various steering committees and working parties.

For address to contact, see Appendix.

School Visits Visits made by the entire school or by individual classes or sets of classes to some place of interest: a museum, theatre, film, the countryside, factories, or even trips abroad. Parental permission is normally first sought for such visits or outings, and teachers accompanying the party are usually held responsible for the safety of their charges. Details of what these responsibilities are and on insurance of children on visits with schools may be obtained from the School Journey Association of London (address listed in Appendix).

Scottish Institute of Adult Education A voluntary body which encourages adult education in Scotland. Numerous bodies, including the Scottish universities and education authorities, are affiliated to it and supply funds. It also receives a grant from the Scottish Education Department.

For address to contact, see Appendix.

See: Adult Education; National Institute for Adult Education; Workers' Educational Association.

Scottish Union of Students (SUS) Founded in 1888, when it was known as the Federation of Scottish University Student Representative Councils, the SUS admitted colleges in 1945. With few exceptions, most Scottish colleges and universities are affiliated to the SUS, which, like the NUS, represents its members on national issues, such as grants, welfare and other educational and political issues.

For address to contact, see Appendix.

Secondary Reorganization See Reorganization.

Secretary of State A Government post of Cabinet rank where education and science are concerned. The Secretary's duties involve: the promotion of the education of the people by deciding the nations' educational policy in accordance with his or her political party's manifesto; action as the nation's spokesman on education; the running of the Department of Education and Science; dealing with questions in Parliament, and negotiating with teaching and other educational unions, associations and sundry pressure groups.

See: Minister of State; Ministers of Education.

Setting The division into different groups or sets of pupils according to their various abilities in any given subject. It differs from streaming in that individuals from different classes or streams in the same age groups are taught certain subjects together. For example, if some pupils in 2A, 2B and 2C are particularly bright at mathematics, they will be brought together for a mathematics lesson more advanced than the remainder of their classes. Similarly, those backward at the subject could also be given special lessons while the remainder of average pupils will be given the 'normal' lesson.

See: Banding; Streaming.

Sex Education Lessons in sexual matters, originally concerned purely with teaching children about the reproductive organs and how babies are produced. Now, it takes in just about the entire gamut of sex, including love-making, homosexuality, contraception, abortion and the emotions experienced. Some schools start such instruction for children as young as eight or nine, others not until the children reach puberty. Not all children are ready to accept the intimate details of sex until they are well into their teens and many parents are objecting against giving such lessons too early and in too much detail. The BBC has produced a number of sex education programmes for both parents and schools on radio, television and radio-vision (a combination of slides or film strips and taped commentaries).

Further reading: *Sex Education in the Primary School* by A. Chanter (Macmillan, 1966); *Teenagers and Parents* by J. Pike (Gollancz, 1965); *A Textbook of Sex Education* by J. Dawkins (Blackwell, 1967).

See: Health Education; Personal Relationships.

Single Sex Schools See Co-education.

Sixth Form The final and most senior class of a secondary school, normally entered by pupils at the age of sixteen-plus, following their sitting and passing of the Ordinary level (O-level) examinations of the General Certificate of Education, or obtaining good grades in the Certificate of Secondary Education (CSE). In the sixth form, students may follow courses leading to Advanced level (A-level) qualifications, which are usually required to enter a university or other establishment of higher education. Many schools still divide their sixth forms into two categories, arts and sciences, allowing students to specialize in one or the other field, but it is now more usual for students to mix arts and science subjects (e.g. history,

English and mathematics; biology, chemistry and a modern language, etc.).

See: Sixth Form College.

Sixth Form College With the development of comprehensive schools it was found necessary to offer a wide choice of subjects that pupils could take at Advanced level (A-level) in the General Certificate of Education (GCE). Since many comprehensive schools, due to their small size (600 to 800 pupils), found it difficult to produce a big sixth form on the premises, some local authorities decided to build a separate college to be shared by the sixth form pupils of several, even all secondary schools in the area. Such junior colleges are now rapidly developing, particularly since it has been almost universally agreed that big comprehensives (1200-plus) face many problems (such as disciplinary difficulties and sheer lack of compactness and identity). Sixth form colleges are also cheaper to run in the long term, since they avoid the need of duplicating expensive laboratories, equipment and teachers in the various schools of the same area or town. However, they also have their disadvantages. Graduate teachers generally demand the opportunity of teaching some Advanced-level classes and are loath to apply to secondary schools that have no sixth form of their own. Thus, children in such schools are often deprived teaching by the more highly qualified teachers.

Further reading: *The Sixth Form College* (Assistant Masters' Association).

See: Comprehensive Education; Sixth Form.

Slow Learners Children who fall below their chronological age in learning; generally those of low IQ who require special education either in special schools for ESN children or in ordinary school remedial classes.

Further reading: *Teaching the Slow Learner* by M. F. Cleugh (Methuen, 1961); *No Child is Ineducable* by S. Segal (Pergamon Press, 1967).

See: Educationally Subnormal; Remedial Classes.

Society of Headmasters of Independent Schools (SHMIS) Membership of this body is open to good secondary schools in the independent sector without the special reservations on the size of sixth forms laid down by the Headmasters' Conference (HMC).

See: Headmasters' Conference (HMC).

Society of Teachers Opposed to Physical Punishment (STOPP) An organization of teachers whose aim is to impose a national ban on all forms of corporal punishment in schools through-out the country. It asks parents to write to their local education authority withdrawing their permission from teachers to act *in loco parentis*, thereby preventing them from physically punishing their children. A number of parents are also members of STOPP.

For address to contact, see Appendix.

See: Corporal Punishment; Punishment.

Special Education Local authorities are required to provide special educational facilities for children who are suffering from any of a number of handicaps. About 130,000 such children exist. Most of them are rated educationally subnormal (ESN), or are maladjusted or have physical handicaps that make it difficult for them to be educated in normal schools. Others are blind or partially sighted, deaf or have seriously impaired hearing. Some suffer from epilepsy, have bad speech defects, are considered very delicate or are autistic. There is a growing movement that wants to see many of the above categories of children fully integrated into normal schools. However, there is an argument against this, as insufficient teachers have been trained to cope with special education. It certainly requires very specialized training to teach the blind, the deaf and the severely physically or mentally handicapped children.

See: Educationally Subnormal; Special Schools.

Special Schools Schools for handicapped pupils. There are nearly 1500 special schools in England and Wales, including 401 boarding schools, as well as 155 hospital schools. There are also about 1300 special classes in ordinary maintained schools catering for about 14,300 full-time and 1000 part-time pupils.

See: Special Education.

Spelling Like reading, spelling has become a very controversial topic. Some of the modern educators say that it does not matter if a child cannot spell properly as long as he manages to express himself on paper fairly fluently. There is certainly a time when teachers should overlook poor spelling in order not to discourage children from writing, particularly at an early age when writing is a new experience. However, once a child has gained confidence in com-position, spelling should gradually be corrected. One of the best methods is to mark the word wrongly spelled and ask the child to write the word correctly, possibly several times, at the end of the corrected piece of writing. Children should be encouraged to look words up in dictionaries (far too few children are actually taught how to use a dictionary or encyclopedia) not only for their correct spelling but also for their definition. Often, children will transpose letters, so that 'on' might become 'no' or 'was' might be written as 'saw'. This is normal at an early age (six to eight) and can be corrected by reasonable remedial teaching. If the fault persists and if the child also reads words in this way, the teacher or parent could suspect the child to be dyslexic (though it would be a mistake to jump to this conclusion too readily).

Spelling taught too soon and too strictly could have a harmful effect on the child. Left too late, on the other hand, it could be equally harmful. Good teachers know at what stage a pupil's bad spelling must be corrected. A child of twelve who still spells like an eight-year-old must not only be corrected but given remedial help, whereas an eight-year-old who spells like a seven-year-old is likely to outgrow this phase.

Advertisers have much to answer for where bad spelling is concerned. 'Drinka-Pinta-Milka-Day' or 'Beenz Meenz Heinz' might make copy-writers pat themselves on their backs, but their clever-clever slogans are a disservice to education.

Parents, however, would do well to remember that the English language consists of no more than forty different sounds but that these may be written in more than 2000 different ways with the use of the conventional 26-letter alphabet. George Bernard Shaw tried to simplify spelling by inventing an alphabet containing forty letters. Sir James Pitman supports Shaw, and has invented his own alphabet of forty-two letters to simplify the learning of reading. Bearing all this in mind, spelling among young children should not be regarded too severely.

Further reading: *In Spite of the Alphabet* by H. Diak (Chatto and Windus, 1965); *The Essentials of Teaching and Testing Spelling* by F. E. Schonell (Macmillan, 1965); *Diagnostic and Remedial Teaching* by G. M. Blair (Collins-Macmillan, 1956); *Instant Reading* by M. Harrison (Pitman, 1964); *The ita Symposium*, edited by W. D. Walls (National Foundation for Educational Research, 1967); *Give Your Child a Chance* by B. Kemble (W. H. Allen, 1970).

See: Dyslexia; Initial Teaching Alphabet (ita).

Streaming The method of placing children into various groups or classes in accordance with their age, aptitude and ability. Despite a number of research studies, it has yet to be proved whether streaming is an advantage or a disadvantage. Most teachers appear to favour streaming as it makes for more uniformity in the classroom. But there are growing factions that prefer classes of a mixture of pupils of all abilities. A streamed school, for example, would place all children aged twelve in two, three or more classes, so that all twelve-year-olds of high ability might find themselves in the A-stream or Form 2A, while those of average ability would be placed in the B-stream (2B) and those of below average ability in the C-stream (2C). Some comprehensives try to hide such obvious A, B and C categories by giving classes less conspicuous letters (2H, 2P, 2M) or names.

See: Setting.

Student Fees Until September 1977, home-based students (i.e. British students or those considered British through residence in this country) paid tuition fees for degree courses at universities or postgraduate courses at the rate of £182 a year, while overseas students paid £416 a year.

But from that date fees were raised by almost phenomenal percentage rates. The home-based students' tuition fees rose to £500 (undergraduate) and £750 (postgraduate), while overseas students had to pay £650 (undergraduate) and £850 (postgraduate).

British students, with comparatively few exceptions, are not affected by this increase of up to 313 per cent, since their fees are automatically paid by local authorities. Thousands of overseas students *were* affected, since many of them have to pay fees out of their own pockets (or their parents'). The (Labour) Government was accused of imposing a quota on foreign students coming into the country and university vice-chancellors protested to the Government and set up 'hardship funds' at their universities to help students in financial distress.

Student Grants Financial assistance given in the form of awards by central or local government to help students with study or research. Awards fall into a number of categories, including postgraduate state studentships, which are on a competitive basis, and postgraduate teacher training awards for graduates following a one-year course of teacher training at a university department of education. There are also the awards made to postgraduate students by the five Research Councils in the form of studentships and fellowships or bursaries. But by far the most important number of grants fall into the three following categories:

Mandatory Grants These are mostly paid by the Government through local education authorities to students on full-time degree courses, teacher training courses, and some (few) diploma courses at polytechnics and further education colleges.

From September 1977, students on first degree courses at London University and other higher education establishments in the capital, received a maximum grant of £1145 a year, while those in the provinces (including Oxford and Cambridge) received a maximum of £1010. Students living at home receive £785. Grants are reviewed annually and are liable to changes.

Postgraduates Grants, also as of September 1977, were as follows: those in London: £1655 a year; those elsewhere: £1475; those living at home: £1075.

All students on mandatory (first degree) grants are able to obtain a minimum maintenance grant of £80 a year (compared with £50 prior to September 1977). All above figures for grants are maxima. Grants for dependent students are calculated according to parental earnings and there is a means test based on the parents' residual income (See residual income). The maximum grant can be obtained if the parental residual income falls below £3200 a year.

Grants as well as the threshold of parental incomes (means test) are generally reviewed annually by the Government (usually in the period around March–May) and are liable to changes.

Students can escape the means test trap which determines the size of their grant and become eligible for the maximum if:

a) they have reached the age of twenty-five either before the start of or during their full-time degree course or –

b) have worked and supported themselves financially (i.e. independent of their parents) for at least three years *prior* to the start of the course.

It has been estimated that out of a total of 390,000 students who are eligible for mandatory grants, about 130,000 are in receipt of the full (maximum) award and about 19,000 receive only the minimum of £80.

Mature students (those aged twenty-six and over or those who have worked for three years prior to the start of their course) receive additional payments on their grants – £100 for every year over twenty-five to a maximum of £400 payable at age twenty-nine. This is an attempt to attract more mature students into higher education.

Discretionary Grants Financial assistance, made at the discretion of local education authorities, to students following non-degree courses (such as ONC, OND, HNC etc.) at colleges of further and higher education. Some authorities are more generous than others and pay 'full value awards', covering the full cost of fees and maintenance in the same way as for mandatory grants. But generally, local authorities are reluctant to make more than a gesture of financial goodwill, particularly at times of economic stringency.

Teacher-training Grants All fees are paid automatically for all mandatory award-holding students who are training to be teachers. Students at colleges which provide free food and lodging do not, however, qualify for the £80 minimum award for maintenance. All other teacher-training students (i.e. those who live in lodgings or in colleges that do not provide free food and accommodation) do qualify for the £80 minimum.

Full details about individual grants and the different types of awards, as well as expert advice, may be obtained from the National Union of Students and/or the Department of Education and Science, Student Awards Branch.

For addresses, see Appendix.

Further reading: *Grants Handbook*, obtainable from the National Union of Students; *Grants for Higher Education* by J. Booth, published by the Advisory Centre for Education; *Grants to Students*, three free booklets (1. courses for which mandatory grants are awarded; 2. grants for student teachers; 3. state bursary schemes) obtainable from the Department of Education and Science; *Grants to Students 4.* (also from the DES) concerns competitive state studentships in the humanities; *Statistics of Education, Vol. 5: Finance and Awards*, with full details of numbers and amounts of awards authority by authority, published annually by the DES (HMSO); *Scottish Educational Statistics* gives details of awards in Scotland, published annually by the Scottish Office (HMSO).

See: Mature State Scholarships; Residual Income; Student Fees.
SUS See Scottish Union of Students.
Suspension Ordering a child to stay away from school as a punishment for an offence committed by the child. Suspension normally spans two days to a week but can last longer. Parents have to be informed immediately of the head's decision to suspend a child and of their right to appeal. The suspension order has to be approved by the school's board of governors, in the case of a secondary school, or by the managers and a subcommittee of the education committee within the local education authority.

Pupils are generally not suspended unless their offence is considered to be a very serious breach of discipline or school rules. Extreme disregard of authority, violence, theft, vandalism and habitual and nasty bullying could lead to suspension. Heads have the moral duty to consider whether the damage done to the school or to pupils in it would be greater by not suspending an individual or group of individuals than the harm done to the offender(s) by ordering the suspension.

Parents may appeal against the order to the governors and/or the local authority. They can demand that their child be sent to another school. If under sixteen, it is still the local authority's duty to provide the child with education.

See: Expulsion.

Sustentation Fund Originally this was a fund collected to help support poverty-stricken members of the clergy. Now, it has been adopted to describe the fund kept by some teacher unions to support members who are in need of financial 'sustenance'. In reality, it serves mainly to keep the 'wolf from the door' of teachers on official strike – hence, it is a strike fund.

T

Tameside One of the boroughs within the Greater Manchester area (it covers fairly industrial towns like Ashton-under-Lyne, Denton, Droylsden, Dukinfield and Hyde) which made political history in 1976. It was a Labour-controlled authority until the local elections of May 1976, when it fell to the Conservatives. Plans to go comprehensive in September of the same year had already been agreed and all was ready for the transition. But the Conservatives claimed that they had been elected because their manifesto had stated that they would reverse the Labour plan. And this they did.

The then Education Secretary, Fred Mulley, sought an order in the High Court under Section 68 of the 1944 Education Act accusing the authority of acting unreasonably. He won. But the authority appealed and the Appeal Court, under Lord Denning and the two other judges, upheld the appeal. A counter-appeal by Mr Mulley to the House of Lords also failed. Tameside had set a sensational precedent and was able, for the time being at least, to keep its selective schools. It was embarrassing for Fred Mulley and, shortly afterwards, he moved to another Ministry (Defence).

Taylor Report See School Government.

Teachers' Centres With the growing need for in-service training of teachers, centres have spread throughout the country where teachers may meet, talk and learn together about new methods in education, in teaching and in the administration of schools. There are now several hundred such centres. Some of them are attached to or form part of large schools, while others stand on their own. They have varying support from local education authorities and are still viewed with some suspicion by administrators and teachers alike. But their potential value and importance is unquestionable and some have become so popular that their size has proved inadequate for the number of teachers wishing to use them.

Further reading: *Teachers' Centres*, edited by R. Thornbury (Darton, Longman & Todd, 1973).

See: In-service Training; Teacher Training.

Teacher Training Whatever criticisms can be launched against the training of teachers, Britain's system of teacher education is still considered to be one of the best in the Western world. The old two-year course at a college of education, which led to the award of a teacher's certificate, was expanded to three years by 1960 with the post-war birth 'bulge' and the need for more and better qualified teachers. At the colleges, student teachers are taught both the theory and the practice of teaching; many colleges specialize in certain teaching fields – physical education, mathematics, home economics, crafts, mature students and so on. Graduates from universities wishing to enter the teaching profession study for an extra year in a university department of education or at a college of higher education. All students are required to gain practical experience in the classroom under the supervision of an experienced teacher. Few other countries provide this practical side to training. With the closures and mergers of many colleges of education in 1981, and the contraction of the number of teacher training places, training is undergoing radical changes. Such changes are likely to improve the quality of teaching as its quantity diminishes.

Further reading: *Education: A Framework for Expansion* (Report of the James Committee, Cmnd 5174, HMSO, 1972); *Children and their Primary Schools* – the Plowden Report (HMSO, 1967); *The Training of Teachers: A Factual Survey*, edited by S. Hewett (University of London Press, 1971); *The First Year of Teaching* by C. Hannam, P. Smyth, N. Stephenson (Penguin, 1976); *Teachers in Turmoil* by V. Burke (Penguin, 1971); *Learning to Teach* by B. Thompson (Sidgwick & Jackson, 1973).

See: B.Ed.; Block Practice; Colleges of Education; James Committee; Teachers' Centres.

Teacher Training Colleges See Colleges of Education.

Teacher Training Grants See Student Grants.

Teaching Practice Experience in the classroom for the student teacher, now also known as classroom experience. Some colleges have their own schools; most have schools in catchment areas which will accept their students for such practice periods. Many of the colleges run courses on the theory of teaching concurrently with periods inside the schools, while some few allow students to do their practical course for up to a term. The latter is known as block practice.

See: Block Practice; Teacher Training.

Team Teaching A method of teaching large groups of children at the same time by several teachers working in small groups. The idea is that the whole group, which could consist of as many as 100 pupils, is addressed by one of the teachers – either a 'master teacher' or even a teacher/lecturer on television – who introduces the theme or theory. This is then discussed in more detail by the smaller groups of children under one of the team of teachers. The subject is planned in detail by the team before the lesson. Team teaching can be useful, for it gives children a chance to hear different aspects of the same subject from a variety of teachers. It is essential that the team is composed of good individual teachers, each an experienced exponent of the subject concerned.

Further reading: *Team Teaching* by K. Lovell (Leeds University Press, 1967).

Technical Colleges These are colleges of further education which offer a wide spectrum of courses in professional and vocational education. Usually referred to as 'techs', they admit students on full-time, part-time or evening course levels, and are found both locally and regionally. The most advanced technical colleges are the polytechnics, as well as some of the technical universities (e.g. Brunel, City) which were formed out of the old CATs (colleges of advanced technology). In all, there are more than 800 such techs in the country. Details of each, together with the courses obtainable and the qualifications that may be gained there, are contained in the *Directory of Further Education* published by the Careers Research and Advisory Centre (CRAC).

Further reading: *Yearbook of Technical Education and Training* (George Godwin, 1975); *Compendium of Advanced Courses in Technical*

Colleges (published annually by the Regional Advisory Councils for Technological Education; address listed in Appendix.

See: CRAC.

Ten-year Rule This ruling, which defined 'immigrant pupil', was dropped after the Conservative Government of 1973 decided to abandon the collection of statistics on immigrant pupils by the Department of Education and Science, then under Mrs Margaret Thatcher. These statistics, which had been introduced in 1966, defined immigrant pupils as:

'children born outside the British Isles who have come to this country with, or to join, parents or guardians whose countries of origin were abroad;' and

'children born in the United Kingdom to parents whose countries of origin were abroad and who came to the UK on or after 1 January, ten years before the collection of the information.'

The ten-year rule, chosen arbitrarily because it was felt that ten years was sufficient to iron out any difficulties such as linguistic handicaps, came under heavy fire. Although attempts were made by Mrs Thatcher and others to find an alternative definition, they proved fruitless. Following criticisms by the report of the Parliamentary Select Committee on Race Relations in 1973 of the rule and the collection of statistics on immigrant pupils, it was dropped as from 27 November 1973.

See: Immigrant Pupils.

Tertiary College A college catering for all persons wishing to continue their education after the age of sixteen, providing courses for men and women on a part-time, full-time, day or evening basis at non-degree standard. In other words, it could be a further education college at which one could take O and A-levels or the Diploma of Higher Education, the Higher National Diploma or Certificate and other, similar qualifications. Alternatively, the tertiary college could be a college open to all aged sixteen to nineteen where O and A-levels are taken – a glorified sixth form college without entry qualifications, run on strictly comprehensive lines. There are about ten such colleges in the country and there are plans to open more to replace sixth forms in schools with insufficient pupils for A-level courses.

See: Sixth Form College.

Three Rs A generally accepted term for the basics in education: reading, (w)riting and (a)rithmetic. These subjects form the core curriculum of primary schools. Some factions feel that a fourth R should be added to the group: religion – and indeed, religion is a compulsory part of the school curriculum and laid down as such by the 1944 Education Act.

See: Core Curriculum.

Transport, School Local authorities are responsible for the free transport of pupils to and from school if the distance between home and school is two miles or more for a child up to the age of eight or three miles or more for those over the age of eight. It is often difficult to know exactly how this distance is measured but this is generally in accordance with the nearest possible route.

Tripartite System This was the school structure before the reorganization of secondary schooling into all-ability comprehensives. Schools were (and in a number of local authorities still are) divided into three types: grammar schools, which admitted children who had passed the eleven-plus examination and were considered to have the highest academic potential; technical schools, which gave children a predominantly vocational education aimed at preparing them for work in industry, commerce and agriculture; secondary modern schools, whose intake of pupils had failed the eleven-plus, and who were given a general education, usually believed to be, but not necessarily, of a lower academic standard than the education obtained at grammar schools.

See: Comprehensive Education.

Truancy The absence of a pupil from school for no legitimate reason. Truancy rates vary from authority to authority and are generally higher in urban, industrial areas. Some estimates put it as high as one million a day nationally – more than ten per cent of the total school population; spot checks by the Department of Education on one picked day have given estimates as low as three per cent. Neither figure is easily proved as a true reflection of truancy, although there is general agreement that truancy presents a tough problem to schools, parents and local authorities.

Reasons for truancy also vary – from school phobia to fear of bullying and sheer boredom with lessons. In some cases, bright children have truanted because they have fallen under the influence of gangs of extortionists at their school – boys and girls who demand money or threaten a beating. Such rackets lead to petty thieving, fear and eventual truanting. Bullying is among the major causes. Truants tend to hide in places away from the crowds; or they spend their time in cinemas; some, whose parents are both at work, simply stay at home and watch television.

Other truants, particularly those at big comprehensive schools, make sure that they are present when the register is called, then walk out of the school. If caught, they explain that they have been sent home for their tie (if a uniform is worn) or other 'important' pieces of equipment, or dinner money.

What is even more worrying is that many truants 'do a bunk' or 'play hookey' with the full knowledge, even the encouragement, of parents. Nearly one half of parents are aware of their children's truancy according to some surveys.

The police have been brought in to help stamp out truancy in some areas of the country, by stopping children seen wandering the streets, noting their names and addresses and taking them back to school. The reason for police action in this matter is that truants are often responsible for day-time burglaries, shop-lifting and theft of cars. Schools will normally contact the Education Welfare Service once the habitual truants have been identified, so that education welfare officers may visit the culprit's home to discuss the problem with the parents who, in the end, are responsible under the 1944 Education Act for the pupil's regular attendance for full-time education.

See: Absence; Attendance; Attendance Order.

U

UCCA (Universities Central Council on Admissions) A clearing house dealing with admissions of students to universities for full-time first degree and diploma courses. It does not include the B.Ed. course. The Open University does not participate in the scheme. It was set up by the universities in 1961 and is financed by them. It publishes annual reports on the admissions, noting differences and trends, shortage subjects or those that are over-subscribed, and gives full statistical data.

Each applicant must complete a form stating his or her choice of subject for study and the universities preferred in order of preference. These forms, obtainable at schools if applicants are pupils, or from the Central Council offices, must be completed a year before the prospective date of entry to the university.

For address to contact, see Appendix.

See: Central Register and Clearing House Ltd.

UGC See University Grants Committee.

Ultra Vires A Latin phrase meaning beyond one's power or authority. Whereas a citizen may perform any act the law does not forbid, a corporate body may only perform such acts as they are authorized to do. Thus, governors or managers of schools may carry out only such duties as are laid down in their articles of government. If they step outside those articles, by, let us say, spending the school's official funds on one big boozy party, they would be acting *ultra vires*. Student unions may spend the grants received out of public funds on educational matters (financing of student societies, sporting activities, lectures, recitals) but may not donate such funds to, say, the local building workers who have gone on strike, even if such an action has been democratically voted on by the student body. Such *ultra vires* payments were denounced in a court in the early seventies (Baldry v. Sussex University Student Union) as totally outside the union's authority since they were not of an educational nature. Students have since managed to circumvent the law by simply inviting a trade unionist, or other representative of a body the students wanted to finance, to 'lecture' to them. They could then pay him a hefty fee on the pretext that the event was 'educational'.

Underachiever A term for a child whose academic work does not match his potential as determined by his teachers or by an intelligence (IQ) test. A child's IQ might show a high potential, say 130, yet his reading or his mathematics might show a quotient of only 110. He will be said to be underachieving in reading or in mathematics by twenty points. The term is also used for a child whose classroom achievements fall below the average of his peers in the same classroom.

UNESCO (United Nations Educational, Scientific and Cultural Organization) An agency of the United Nations. It promotes mutual understanding and knowledge, educational and cultural progress among the peoples of the world. It was set up in 1945 and first met as a conference in Paris in 1946. It has tried, among other matters, to tackle widespread adult illiteracy, universal primary education and to give greater access to secondary and higher education. It has an executive board of thirty members and is financed by member states in proportion to their wealth (America contributes nearly one third of the funds, while Britain gives about seven per cent and some developing countries only a fraction of one per cent). It publishes a wide range of books, journals and pamphlets in about twenty-two languages, including the monthly *Courier* (in eight languages).

For address to contact, see Appendix.

Uniforms School uniforms, which originated in the public schools, have become a contentious issue with the rise of egalitarianism in education, and are identified with elitism and selection. Subconsciously, however, the move against the wearing of distinctive blazers, badges, caps, ties and the like is really tied up with finance and inflation. It has simply become a luxury that not many parents wish to buy. There are arguments for and against the wearing of uniforms. A uniform identifies a school and allows children to feel themselves to be part of that school. It also has an equalizing effect in that, it is said, one cannot differentiate between a rich child and one from a poorer home background. On the other hand, whereas the pupil from a rich home can probably afford two uniforms, thus always looking neat (and rich), the poor child's sole uniform might become tatty after a while. It also means more work for the parent who has to keep the uniform clean and well pressed. Children tend to favour uniforms, at least up to the senior forms, and if the school has no uniform rule, they often invent one (jeans and denim jackets are rapidly becoming the uniform among youngsters at such schools). Schools that insist on uniforms would be wise to keep them simple and of the kind which can be bought at chain or department stores at reasonable cost, particularly shirts and blouses with pullovers, skirts and trousers that are easy to wash (drip-dry) and are hard-wearing and of colours that do not dirty easily (grey, green, brown – almost anything other than white).

See: Financial Aid.

Unions There are at present more than 500,000 serving teachers in the United Kingdom. About 431,000 of these are in schools in England and Wales alone, most of them (about 173,000 men and 258,000 women) in state-maintained primary and secondary schools. As a profession, teachers form what must be considered the most highly organized group of white-collar workers in the country. And yet they are very seriously split.

No fewer than nine associations or unions exist for teachers. Eight of these are represented on the Burnham Committee, which negotiates salaries (the odd one out being the Professional Association of Teachers – PAT – which was formed in 1970 of teachers who refused to go along with the militancy of some of the other unions and pledged themselves never to strike. PAT has now some 11,000 members).

The 'Big Two' are without any doubt the National Union of Teachers (NUT) which claims 232,000 in-service (i.e. actually teaching) members, and the National Association of Schoolmasters/ Union of Women Teachers (NAS/UWT) which in November 1977 claimed 100,000 members. The UWT was formed in 1965 and later merged with the NAS. Both these unions boast constantly increasing membership figures. Considering that as many as 90,000 teachers belong to no union at all and the total number of teachers claimed as members of all nine unions comes to well over 450,000, there is clearly either some deception in their claims or there are many thousands of teachers with dual membership.

The Joint Four, comprising the Assistant Masters Association, the Association of Assistant Mistresses, the Association of Head-mistresses and the Headmasters' Association, has in the region of 70,000 members in all, while the National Association of Head Teachers (NAHT) which, represents roughly two-thirds of all state-maintained primary and secondary schools, has more than 19,000 members. Finally, the National Association of Teachers in Further and Higher Education (NATFHE), whose members are in colleges of education, polytechnics and colleges of further education, represents in the region of 40,000 such teachers.

The greatest rivalry exists between the NUT and the NAS/UWT, who appear to squabble constantly on numerous issues, but particularly about their respective membership figures. This is not so much because the NAS/UWT challenges the NUT's undoubted claim to being the country's biggest teachers' union, but because it is opposed to the NUT's equally undoubted monopoly of negotiations, particularly in the Burnham Committee. It is there that the NUT has an overall majority – sixteen members – compared with the NAS/UWT's three members, the NAHT's solitary one, the Joint Four's six and NATFHE's two. The latter is closely related to the NUT and usually votes with the union. But even without NATFHE's two votes, the NUT has four votes more than all the others put together.

The NAS/UWT claims, with some justice, that even if the NUT's figure of 232,000 in-service members were correct, this would make the NUT only 2.4 times as big as the rival body. To have 5.3 times as many members on Burnham as the NAS/UWT would, it says, seem somewhat unfair.

But whatever the true figures for all the unions are, the unions themselves are all excellently organized with highly efficient officers in modern offices using the latest equipment, including computers, to help them run their affairs smoothly on behalf of their members. Each offers its members legal advice and assistance and defends them in respect of claims made against them by parents or others as well as protecting them against threats from their employers (the local authorities). Each also offers insurance schemes, including those for life, property, travel and motor cars and many of them also run advantageous travel services, special discount facilities at shops, stores, hotels and the like, and a teachers' benevolent fund for those members in need of emergency loans. The NUT even has its own building society to provide a house purchasing service exclusively for its members. All the unions publish their own journals (*The Teacher*, official organ of the NUT appears weekly except for a brief spell during the summer holidays).

Each union runs its annual conference (and many also organize interim conferences on a variety of educational matters) at which policies, fresh demands and grievances are aired.

It is mainly due to the work and constant nagging of the unions that teachers salaries have been raised, that class sizes have been reduced, that general conditions both for them and for their pupils have been improved. Several of them have 'friends', even members in both Houses of Parliament (the NUT has as many as thirty MPs in membership of the union) and have ready access to the Secretary of State for Education – who usually listens to their demands.

Burnham is not the only body on which these organizations are represented. They also have a powerful voice within the Schools Council and sit on countless inquiries producing endless reports. The NAS/UWT even has a special training centre at Rednal, near Birmingham, where it trains its officers in the art of negotiating pay settlements and organizing yet more members.

Yet despite all this expertise and despite constant demands from members to establish union unity under a single umbrella, most of them agree to disagree and stay very much apart. It is a matter of divided they stand, united they fall – or so their leaders seem to fear.

United Nations University An international 'task force' of academics from the universities of countries throughout the world who meet to discuss and try to solve world-wide problems, such as hunger, pollution, birth control, etc. Its headquarters are in Tokyo, and it was set up by the gathering of seventy experts in the autumn of 1975. The University has a high-powered administration under Dr James M. Hester, Rector.

For address to contact, see Appendix.

Universities These are independent, degree-awarding institutions of higher education, the oldest having been founded in the Middle Ages (Oxford's University College was established in 1249, and Cambridge's Peterhouse was founded in 1284) while the newest, the Open University, first opened its doors via radio and television in 1971. Including the latter, there are forty-six universities in England, Wales, Scotland and Northern Ireland.

Apart from the Open University, the newest universities are Sussex, founded in 1961, York (1963), East Anglia (1963), Essex (1964), Kent (1965), Warwick (1965), Lancaster (1964). The colleges of advanced technology (CATs), set up in 1956, were also granted university status (technical universities) following the Robbins Report of 1963. For example, the City of London Northampton College became City University, the Welsh CAT became the University of Wales Institute of Science and Technology. The Universities of Aston in Birmingham, Brunel, Bath, Loughborough and Surrey were all CATs.

Most universities are founded by Royal Charter and are autonomous institutions, while others, equally autonomous, were set up by Act of Parliament. The London School of Economics, part of London University, is actually a limited company.

Further reading: *Patterns and Policies in Higher Education* by G. Brosan and others (Penguin Education Special, 1971).

See: Civic University; Federal University; Open University; Robbins Report.

University Entrance Requirements Universities usually impose two sets of requirements on prospective candidates. The general requirement is designed to ensure that candidates have an education of sufficient breadth. It usually consists of a minimum number of GCE O-level and A-level passes (e.g. three O-levels and two A-levels, two O-levels and three A-levels). The passes normally must include certain specific subjects: English, a foreign language and mathematics and/or a science are frequently required. Grades are taken into consideration as well as the number and subjects of passes.

Most universities are prepared to consider candidates with qualifications other than the specified GCE or SCE passes, e.g. ONC, OND, HNC, HND.

In addition to satisfying the general requirement, applicants for many subjects must pass certain A and O-level subjects to ensure that they have an appropriate foundation for further study; thus, most prospective medical students will be expected to have passes in three A-level science subjects.

Compendium of University Entrance Requirements, a comprehensive list of first degree courses at universities in Britain, is published annually by the Association of Commonwealth Universities (address listed in Appendix). The general entrance requirement of each university and the specific subject requirements for individual courses are given.

University Grants Committee (UGC) Founded in 1919, this committee comprises twenty members, most of them academics, who advise the Government on university matters. The Government awards a block grant to the committee, which then shares it out among the universities in accordance with their particular needs. This grant used to be made on a five-yearly basis but in recent years, owing to the rapid rate of inflation, the grant is generally awarded on an annual basis.

For address to contact, see Appendix.

V

Vandalism One third of all vandalism in Britain's schools is committed by children aged under twelve. Acts of vandalism and arson cost the country more than £15,000,000 a year at 1976 prices. Vandalism in Glasgow alone is equivalent to the cost of two new primary schools a year. In 1972–3, schools in the United States spent the same amount of money on losses incurred through vandalism and security services on school campuses as the entire subcontinent spent on textbooks. According to research in the Manchester area, only three per cent of cases of vandalism are likely to find their way into official records.

The above statistics are culled from a survey published in 1977 by the Save the Children Fund. It found that girls were becoming even more destructive than boys. Vandalism can range from windows deliberately smashed by children, to the wanton destruction of entire classrooms, daubing paint on walls, destroying laboratory equipment and expensive audio-visual aids, and the burning down of schools. Many of the reasons for such behaviour are the same as for general violence.

To counteract vandalism, schools require better counselling services, improved relations between pupils and teachers, and better facilities for leisure activity. Pupils should be given the responsibility of keeping their classes and equipment in good condition, thus encouraging an attitude of protectiveness towards communal property.

A system of rewards in return for certain duties can also reduce damage. Parents should be consulted here and asked to co-operate. For example, children who attended every lesson for a month could be taken to the theatre, cinema, football match or other special occasion they enjoy. This would help reduce truancy. Similar incentives could be introduced for the proper use of school equipment, tidiness, punctuality, etc.

One school in Essex, a big comprehensive, introduced a time-clock of the kind that is used in factories for fifth formers. Each pupil had to clock in and clock out at the end of the day. Each received a fictitious wage per week; overtime was paid for after-school activities, ranging from football to society meetings. At the end of the week, pupils had to calculate their own pay-packets, deducting income tax, insurance and specified amounts for every period of five minutes late. Not only did this method teach children about the world of work, it also radically reduced truancy and promoted punctuality.

Further reading: *Vandalism in Schools* by J. Stone and F. Taylor (Save the Children Publications, 1977); *Helping Troubled Children* by M. Rutter (Penguin, 1975); *Vandalism*, edited by C. Ward (Architectural Press, 1963).

See: Violence.

Vice-Chancellor Although the term implies that its holder is 'deputy to the Chancellor', he is, in fact, the head or principal of a university, discharging all its administrative functions. The 'V-C' presides over most senior committees and performs all the functions of a managing director of a high-powered industry. Scottish universities spell out the post and its responsibilities more clearly by calling it 'Principal and Vice-Chancellor'. Vice-Chancellors have their own representative 'umbrella' body (See: Vice-Chancellors and Principals of the Universities of the UK, Committee of).

Vice-Chancellors and Principals of the Universities of the UK, Committee of (CVCP) A body representing the interests of all universities and speaking on behalf of the universities to other groups, including the Government, industry and commerce. All vice-chancellors and principals are members and there are numerous sub-committees dealing with separate academic, financial and administrative matters. Its chairman is elected. In recent years the committee has played an increasingly active role in arguing against Government cuts and pointing out the dangers such cuts spell for the future of universities in general.

For address to contact, see Appendix.

Violence There can be little doubt that violence in schools is on the increase, though it would be wrong to suggest that it is a totally new phenomenon. Surveys by the National Association of Schoolmasters have highlighted cases of both physical and verbal violence on the part of pupils towards other pupils and teachers, as well as assaults by parents on teachers. The obvious question to be asked is why such acts of aggression are on the increase. The answer is not a simple one but entails a whole collection of different causes. The following are meant as just a few possible pointers.

Television Although survey after survey has failed to connect school violence with the violence shown in television programmes, one need only look at a normal playground fight today and compare it with such a fight, say twenty years ago, to find some TV influence. Then, children would fight by punching each other or wrestling. Today, it does not take long before one or the other antagonist 'puts the boot in'. There is the 'kung-fu' kick and the karate chop. Knives and other weapons are drawn. But television has another, far more pernicious, influence. It is simply that children watch it a great deal. The very act of sitting still for hours on end, hypnotized by the little screen, stultifies a child's normal energy. Somehow that energy must be released. Often, it is released in the classroom and in the playground, in the form of shouting (noise is a form of violence that disrupts many classes) or more physical violence. Language itself is violently used on television, with swearing occurring in programmes even in the early evening, and many such programmes depict a fight against authority. Thus, swearing in the class and at teachers become a reflection of what the child hears and sees.

Crime Crime rates within society have risen rapidly, particularly crimes of violence against persons and the abuse of property. In 1972, police records showed that 25,000 burglaries had been committed by youngsters aged between ten and seventeen; by 1975 this figure had almost doubled to 46,000. Of all those found guilty of terrorist offences including murder, in Northern Ireland in 1975, sixty-five per cent were aged under twenty-one. Muggings, rape, vandalism and arson have all increased by leaps and bounds over the past several years – the main offenders: teenagers. It is little wonder that such statistics are also reflected in the schools.

Divorce The number of divorces and separations has reached record proportions in Britain. With verbal and physical violence committed in the home between fathers and mothers, it would be little short of miraculous if children remained unaffected. There are now some one million children living in single-parent families. And that does not take into consideration the many hundreds of thousands of children whose parents have not separated, but who spend their days and nights rowing. Without parental love, the home can easily become the breeding ground for violence. It is often a desperate cry for help, of wanting to be noticed – even if that attention means some form of punishment. Punishment is frequently regarded by such children as being preferable to being completely ignored.

Size The size of many of our comprehensive schools often means they are too big to have any kind of real identity. What chance have the children in a school of, say, 2000 pupils, if the teachers in that school do not even know each other? A big campus, possibly on two or more sites, leads to equally grandiose disciplinary problems, including truancy. It is almost impossible to control misbehaviour on a huge campus or to notice which children have 'gone over the wall' to play truant if there is constant movement between classes and groups, especially between separate sites. In the case of very big schools, division into different houses is advisable.

Teacher Militancy Very few children can by now be unaware of the wave of unrest among teachers, whose unions have, with every justification, fought against oversized classes, poor conditions and cuts in educational resources, and campaigned for higher salaries. Most children, indeed, are aware of what their teachers are earning and some have probably seen Miss or Sir demonstrating in the streets. Because of teachers' strikes, the profession, once among the most respected, has placed itself on the same level as dockers, printers, miners and other workers. Not that there is anything wrong in that, but militancy among teachers tends to rub off on pupils.

Teaching Methods Modern progressive teaching methods have often been undertaken by inexperienced, ill-informed teachers, who have interpreted 'discovery' and other, similar philosophies as 'do-as-you-please'. Without a proper structure in the classroom, discipline disintegrates and disruption and violence follow close at heel.

Economy It is difficult to explain to youngsters whose fathers or brothers are out of work, that examinations and qualifications are vital. At a time of high unemployment, when parents are constantly complaining about the high cost and lower standards of living, and when tempers start flaring in the home about the household budget, children are bound to start wondering what education and schools are all about. This general malaise can easily lead to a 'to-hell-with-it' attitude, particularly among teenagers, and emerge as violence.

Materialism Somehow, the list has come full circle and is back to television again. Despite unemployment, despite inflation, despite strikes and wages stand-stills, commercial television continues to lull viewers into a belief that all is Technicolor beauty and truth. Advertisers persuade families that they cannot possibly live without this or the other gadget, that by biting into a certain chocolate bar they will instantly be transported to a beautiful desert island, or that by eating another, they will experience an orgasm of delight. This kind of cloud-cuckoo-land of materialism can have the most disastrous effects on the young (and not so young, at that). Some parents will buy gadgets they really cannot afford and do not really need. Some children, who do not have the money in the first place will steal the articles, using violence if necessary.

It is unfair to place all the blame for violence and indiscipline on the schools and expect them somehow to form an oasis of purity in the midst of a desert of violence. Schools form a part of society. If society is immoral, schools, as a reflection of that society, will also contain elements of immorality.

On a recent visit to the United States, I asked the Secretary of State for Education in Washington DC, what had 'gone wrong' in American schools. He replied: 'Once, parents used to give their children time, love and discipline. Today, they give them money.' Far too many parents in Britain also follow this principle. Often they are unaware of what their children are doing, where they are, what television programmes they are watching and how long they spend watching the 'box'. The order: 'Be quiet. I'm busy. Go and watch television,' is heard daily in many a home. The result *can* lead to violence, whether it is translated by the child kicking a tin can along the road or in kicking a teacher in the classroom.

See: Vandalism; Discipline; Corporal Punishment; Rules.

Voluntary Schools These are generally denominational schools – that is, those founded by the Churches. They fall into the following categories:

Voluntary Aided Most of these are Church of England and Roman Catholic foundation schools. The managers or governors are responsible for the outside of the buildings and may alter, enlarge or otherwise improve them. For this they must find fifteen per cent of the finance, the remainder being paid by the Government. The local authority is responsible for all teachers except those dealing solely with religious education and pays their salaries as well as supplying books and equipment. Two thirds of the managers or governors are appointed by the voluntary body and one third by the local authority.

Voluntary Controlled Here, the local authority is responsible for both the inside and the outside of the buildings and appoints two thirds of the managers or governors, while the voluntary body (almost exclusively Church of England) appoints one third. The local authority also appoints the teachers, but must consult the managers or governors over the appointment of the head teacher and any teachers giving religious education.

Special Agreement These are secondary schools and are rather similar to voluntary aided schools. Costs of maintenance are divided between the voluntary body and the local authority, which by special agreement pays between fifty and seventy-five per cent of the building costs. The local authority appoints only one third of the governors, two thirds of them being the voluntary body's appointees. Again, the local authority appoints all teachers other than those dealing with religious education.

It is up to the governors of voluntary secondary schools to decide whether they should scrap selection and become comprehensive. In the case of voluntary aided schools, some local authorities have threatened to withdraw their aid in order to persuade governing bodies to opt for comprehensive status. In view of this threat, a number of such schools have decided to go independent, thereby cutting themselves off entirely from local authority jurisdiction.

Voucher System A system whereby the parent is issued with a voucher to the value of a year's schooling, which he may then present at the school of his choice for the education of his child. In other words, if the normal average cost to the local authority of a place at a school is, say, £500 per year, the voucher will be at that value. Instead of paying the school this *per capita* amount, it is given to the parent who can make his own choice. The system has been tried with success in some parts of the United States (originally at Alum Rock, California) in the late sixties and there is a growing lobby seeking the voucher's introduction in Britain. Supporters believe that the scheme would place schools on a more commercial basis and force them to become more accountable for their educational standards and thus improve these standards. Obviously, a school considered poor by parents would lose business, while those considered good would become over-subscribed. The good schools might have to build extra accommodation to cope with the additional demand; the poor schools might have to close or show an improvement in their standards. That, at least, is the theory.

There are numerous ways in which the system could be implemented: either for state-maintained schools only, for primary schools only, for secondary schools only or for all schools, including independent schools (in the latter, parents would have to pay the difference between the value of the voucher and the fee from their own pockets). Vouchers in areas of special deprivation could have a slightly higher value than those in 'normal' areas, to allow schools to use the extra money for additional teachers, audio-visual aids or other remedial equipment. Schools in areas adopting such a system would be forced to issue detailed prospectuses of their curricula, teaching methods and aims.

Further reading: *Education for Democrats* by A. Peacock and J. Wiseman (Institute of Economic Affairs, London, 1964); *Education – A Framework for Choice* by A. F. C. Beales, M. Blaug, E. G. West and D. Veal (Institute of Economic Affairs, London, 1967); *Paying for Private Schools* by H. Glennerster and G. Wilson, LSE Studies on Education (Allen Lane, The Penguin Press, 1970).

See: FEVER.

W

Wales, Schools Council Committee for A body dealing primarily with educational and curriculum research for education in Wales and in Welsh language teaching. It produces a number of important pamphlets and books on the subject, including *Teaching through the Medium of Welsh in Secondary Schools in Wales, Sixth Form General Studies in Wales, The Development of Bilingual Education in Wales* and *Welsh – A Programme of Research and Development.*

For address to contact, see Appendix.

WEA See Workers' Educational Association.

Welsh Education This closely resembles the education system in England and, although the Department of Education and Science is responsible for most of the education in Wales, primary and secondary schools are the responsibility of the Secretary of State for Wales. In a number of schools, teaching is carried out in Welsh with English taught as a second language. The Welsh Education Office functions very much along the same lines as the DES. Indeed, it is a miniature replica of it, having its own inspectorate and own branches.

For address to contact, see Appendix.

Further reading: *Education Committees Year Book*, published annually by Councils and Education Press (address listed in Appendix).

See: DES; Education in Scotland.

Welsh Joint Education Committee An advisory body which co-ordinates policies and promotes Welsh views on education, as well as acting as an advisory body for further education in Wales. It also acts as the examining body for both the General Certificate of Education (GCE) and the Certificate of Secondary Education (CSE) in Wales.

For address to contact, see Appendix.

Workers' Educational Association (WEA) Non-party political federation of about 3000 workers' educational organizations, founded in 1903 by Albert Mansbridge, a clerk with the Co-operative Wholesale Society, to encourage workers to take advantage of further education and help develop themselves and their children within society. There are more than 800 branches of the WEA spread throughout the country giving classes in a wide variety of subjects to about 150,000 students. It is recognized by the Department of Education and Science and receives grants from local authorities. It has twenty-one district secretaries.

For address to contact, see Appendix.

See: Adult Education; National Institute of Adult Education; Scottish Institute of Adult Education.

Y

Youth Services Youth services in Britain are a well-organized chain of associations that form a link between the official backing of local education authorities and hard-working, unpaid volunteers. The following are just some of the many that exist:

The National Council for Voluntary Youth Services This council has some forty organizations affiliated to it as well as numerous local bodies that co-ordinate youth services within their individual areas. A selection of member organizations include:

Army Cadet Force Association
58 Buckingham Gate, London SW1E 6AN
Association for Jewish Youth
192–6 Hanbury Street, London E1 5HU
Boys' Brigade
Brigade House, Parsons Green, London SW6
Co-operative Youth Movement
28 Upper Bainbridge Street, Derby DE3 6WN
Girls' Brigade
Brigade House, Parsons Green, London SW6
Girls' Venture Corps
33 St George's Drive, London SW1V 4DH
Jewish Lads' Brigade
192–6 Hanbury Street, London E1 5HU
Methodist Association of Youth Clubs
2 Chester House, Pages Lane, Muswell Hill, London N10 1PR
National Association of Boys' Clubs
17 Bedford Square, London WC1B 3JJ
National Association of Youth Clubs
30 Devonshire Street, London W1N 2AP
National Council for Young Men's Christian Associations
640 Forest Road, London E17 3DZ
National Elfrida Rathbone Society
17 Victoria Park Square, Bethnal Green, London E2 9PE
National Federation of Gateway Clubs
Pembridge Hall, 17 Pembridge Square, London W2 4EP

Girl Guides Association
17–19 Buckingham Palace Road, London SW1W oPT
The Scout Association
Baden-Powell House, Queen's Gate, London SW7 5JS
Union of Maccabi Associations
1 Manchester Square, London W1M 5RF
Woodcraft Folk
13 Ritherdon Road, London SW17 8QE
Young Christian Workers
106 Clapham Road, London SW9 oJX
Young Volunteer Force Foundation
7 Leonard Street, London EC2
Youth Hostels Association
Trevelyan House, 8 St Stephen's Hill, St Albans, Herts AL1 2DY

Scotland

Standing Consultative Council on Youth and Community Service. Founded in 1964 by the Secretary of State for Scotland to promote the youth service and to foster links between the voluntary organizations and the statutory authorities.

Address: Scottish Education Department, St Andrew's House, Edinburgh EH11 3DB.

Scottish Standing Conference of Voluntary Youth Organizations. Has a similar list of organizations in membership as the English National Council's. The following addresses may be useful:

Catholic Youth Council, Bonnington Bank House, 205 Ferry Road, Edinburgh EH6 4NN

Church of Scotland Department of Education, 121 George Street, Edinburgh EH2 4YN

Girl Guides Association of Scotland, 16 Coates Crescent, Edinburgh EH3 7AH

Scout Association, 44 Charlotte Square, Edinburgh EH2 4HQ

Wales

Council for Wales of Voluntary Youth Services, Youth Community Officer, 2 Cathedral Road, Cardiff.

Northern Ireland

Standing Conference of Youth Organizations in Northern Ireland, Education Offices, 40 Academy Street, Belfast BT1 2NQ.

British Youth Council Helps to link the various voluntary youth organizations with the youth sections of the political parties. It represents Britain on the World Assembly of Youth and other international youth movements.

Address: 57 Chalton Street, London NW1 1HU.

National Youth Bureau Founded 1973 and replaced the Youth Service Information Centre. Has teachers and social workers as well as youth workers on its council.

Address: 37 Belvoir Street, Leicester LE1 6SL.

Enterprise Youth Promotes the various voluntary services and assists in finding places within the organizations for volunteers in Scotland.

Address: 29 Queen Street, Edinburgh EH2 1JX.

King George's Jubilee Trust (1935) Its aims are to promote the spiritual and physical welfare of young people aged from fourteen to twenty. The Queen is Patron of the Trust which is based at St James's Palace.

Office Address: 38 Chesham Place, London SW1X 8HA.

The Duke of Edinburgh's Award Set up in 1956, it has become one of the most popular of schemes for young people, providing a wide range of activities to youngsters aged 14–25 in schools, youth organizations, companies and through the Award's various centres. Nearly 1,300,000 young people have competed for its coveted Bronze, Silver and Gold awards, which require competitors to succeed in covering four sections: Service, Personal Interests, Expeditions, and a choice of either Design for Living or Physical Activity. Many of those who have taken part are physically handicapped.

The Award is directed from several offices. Headquarters are:

England: 2 Old Queen Street, London SW1
Scotland: 10 Palmerston Place, Edinburgh 12
Wales: 9 Cathedral Road, Cardiff CF1 9AH
Northern Ireland: 593 Lisburn Road, Belfast BT9 7GS.

International

Council for Volunteers Overseas. An independent, non-Governmental organization advising volunteers from other societies who wish to go abroad, and the Ministry of Overseas Development on matters of policy on volunteer programmes. It was set up in 1964.

Address: 26 Bedford Square, London WC1B 3HU.

International Voluntary Service. Furthers international understanding by bringing different people of various backgrounds, ages and nationalities together in community service. It organizes scores of work-camps in Britain each year and helps send British volunteers to similar camps abroad. One must be sixteen-plus to work in this country and eighteen-plus to go overseas.

Address: 91 High Street, London NW10.

Voluntary Service Overseas (VSO). Founded in 1958, this is among the best known and most effective of overseas volunteer services. It sends graduates and experts particularly to developing countries. It has some 1200 volunteers in 60 countries, most of them in the Third World, the Near and Far East and South America. Teachers, doctors, agricultural workers, architects and accountants figure among its ambassadors abroad. It should be noted that volunteers are usually asked to give their services for two years, although shorter periods are sometimes granted.

Address: 14 Bishop's Bridge Road, London W2 6AA.

Note: There are many other youth services and voluntary organizations that have not been listed here owing to limits of space. Full lists could be obtained from the National Council for Voluntary Youth Services (see first entry above).

Z

Zoning The division of a district into areas from which a given school may draw its pupils. Schools are allocated these areas or zones so that they neither become over-subscribed nor under-used. Local authorities have to give the public full notice of their intention to zone a school or schools. Children already attending a school to be zoned should not be affected. It is often the case that children will have to attend a school which is not the one nearest to their home if that home falls into a zone embracing a different school. With the movement of population it sometimes becomes necessary to abandon a zone, which is also known as a catchment area.

APPENDIX:
Useful Addresses

Adult Education:
National Centre for Adult
   Education
Mr A. K. Stock, Secretary
35 Queen Anne Street
London W1M 0BL

Adventure Playgrounds:
London Adventure Playground
   Association
Capt. D. N. Forbes, Secretary
25 Ovington Square
London SW3 1LQ

Advisory Centre for Education
18 Victoria Park Square
Bethnal Green
London E2 9PF

Agriculture:
Association for Agricultural
   Education Staffs
R. M. Boothroyd
Cumbria College of Agriculture
   and Forestry
Newton Rigg
Penrith
Cumbria CA11 0AH

Association of Agriculture

Miss J. H. D. Bostock,
Victoria Chambers
16-20 Strutton Ground
London SW1P 2HP

AMA (Assistant Master's
   Association)
Mr Andrew Hutchings, CBE,
   MA, Secretary
Gordon House
29 Gordon Square
London WC1H 0PT

Arts Council:
Arts Council of Great Britain
105 Piccadilly
London W1V 0AU

Scottish Arts Council
19–20 Charlotte Square
Edinburgh EH2 4DF

Welsh Arts Council
Holst House
Museum Place
Cardiff CF1 3NX

Assessment of Performance
   Unit (APU)
c/o Department of Education
   and Science

Elizabeth House
York Road
London SE1 7PH

Association of Blind and
    Partially Sighted Teachers
    and Students (ABAPSTAS)
Terry Moody, Secretary
Department of Political
    Economy
Glasgow University
Glasgow G12 8RT

Association of Christian
    Teachers
Mr David G. Blair, Secretary
47 Marylebone Lane
London W1M 6AY

Association of European
    Education Correspondents
John Izbicki, President
The Daily Telegraph
Fleet Street
London EC4

Association of Headmistresses
    (AHM)
Miss L. Spalding, MA,
29 Gordon Square
London WC1H 0PU

Association of Headmistresses
    of Preparatory Schools
    (AHMPS)

Mrs C. M. Leigh, B.Sc.,
Meadowbrook
Abbot's Drive
Virginia Water
Surrey GU25 4QS

Association of University
    Teachers (AUT)
Mr Laurie Sapper
United House
1 Pembridge Road
London W11 3HJ

Autism:
National Society for Autistic
    Children
Mrs M. White, Secretary
1a Golders Green Road
London NW11 8EA

BACIE (British Association for
    Commercial and Industrial
    Education)
16 Park Crescent
London W1N 4AP

British Federation of Music
    Festivals
Mrs Eileen Craine, Secretary
106 Gloucester Place
London W1H 3DB

Careers Advice:
Careers Advisory Service
    (England and Wales)
Department of Employment

(Youth Branch)
97 Tottenham Court Road
London W1P 0ER

(Scotland)
Advisory Committee on Youth
  Employment in Scotland
Stuart House
Semple Street
Edinburgh EH3 8YX

(Northern Ireland)
Youth Employment Service
  Board
46a Howard Street
Belfast BT1 6BH

Careers Teaching:
National Association of Careers
  Teachers (NACT)
Mr L. T. Gray, Secretary
Green Vista
Seale Lane
Seale
Farnham
Surrey

CASE (Confederation for the
  Advancement of State
  Education)
J. D. Pearson, Hon. Secretary
1 Windermere Avenue
Wembley
Middlesex HA9 8SH

Catholic Teachers' Federation
Ald. C. H. Sheill, KSG,
12 Queens Road

Hendon
London NW4

Central Register and Clearing
  House Ltd.
3 Crawford Place
London W1H 2BN

Centre for Educational
  Disadvantage
11 Anson Road
Manchester M14 5BY

Children's Rights Workshop
73 Balfour Street
London SE17

Christian Education Movement
Rev. John M. Sutcliffe,
  Gen. Secretary
2 Chester House
Pages Lane
London N10 1PR

City and Guilds of London
  Institute
76 Portland Place
London W1N 4AA

Consortia:
CFG
Shirehall
Abbey Faregate
Shrewsbury
Salop SY2 6NF

CLASP
County Hall
West Bridgford
Nottingham

CLAW Development Group
Queen's Court
Plymouth Street
Cardiff CF1 4DA

CLEAPSE
ILEA
County Hall
London SE1

Consortium of Method Building
Somerset County Council
County Hall
Taunton

SCOLA
County Hall
Chichester

Correspondence Colleges:
Council for the Accreditation
   of Correspondence Colleges
L. J. Harper, MBE, BA,
   Secretary
27 Marylebone Road
London NW1 5JS

Nalgo Correspondence Institute
Nalgo House
1 Mabledon Place
London WC1H

The National Extension College
131 Hills Road
Cambridge

Pitmans Correspondence
   College
Worcester Road
Wimbledon
London SW19 4DS

Wolsey Hall
Oxford OX2 6PR

Council for National Academic
   Awards (CNAA)
344–54 Gray's Inn Road
London WC1 8BP

CRAC (Careers Research and
   Advisory Centre)
Hobsons Press
Bateman Street
Cambridge CB2 1LZ

Denominational Associations:
The Baptist Union of Great
   Britain and Northern Ireland
Baptist Church House
4 Southampton Road
London WC1B 4AB

British Council of Churches
   Education Unit
10 Eaton Gate
London SW1W 9BT

The Catholic Education Council
41 Cromwell Road
London SW7 2DJ

Central Council for Jewish
   Religious Education
Woburn House (2nd Floor)

Upper Woburn Place
London WC1H 0EP

Central Joint Education Policy
  Committee
69 Great Peter Street
London WC1H 9HH
  and
41 Cromwell Road
London SW7 2DJ

Churches of Christ
59 Vicarage Road
Kings Heath
Birmingham B14 7QA

Church of England Board of
  Education
Church House
Dean's Yard
Westminster
London SW1P 3NZ

Countess of Huntingdon's
  Connexion
Huntingdon Hall
65 De La Warr Road
East Grinstead
West Sussex RH19 3BS

The Free Church Federation
  Council Education Committee
27 Tavistock Square
London WC1 9HH

The Free Church of England
65 Elmfield Avenue
Teddington
Middlesex

Friends Education Council and

Joint Committee
Friends House
Euston Road
London NW1 2BJ

Independent Methodist
  Churches
55 Toothill Road
Loughborough
Leicestershire LE11

Methodist Church (Division
  of Education and Youth)
2 Chester House
Pages Lane
London N10 1PR

Moravian Church
Church House
5 Muswell Hill
London N1 3TJ

Presbyterian Church of Wales
9 Camden Road
Brecon
Powys LD3 7BU

Union of Welsh Independents
11 St Helen's Road
Swansea
Glamorganshire

The United Reformed Church
86 Tavistock Place
London WC1H 9RT

Wesleyan Reform Union
Church House
123 Queen Street
Sheffield S1 2DU

DES (Department of Education and Science):
Department of Education and Science
Elizabeth House
York Road
London SE1 7PH

Education Committees Year Book
Councils and Education Press
5 Bentinck Street
London W1M 5RN

Drink and Drugs
Institute for the Study of Drug Dependence
Mr James Cowley, Chief Officer
Kingsbury House
3 Blackburn Road
London NW6 1XA

Teachers Advisory Council on Alcohol and Drug Education
2 Mount Street
Manchester M2 5NG

Educational Drama Association
Celia Reeves, Hon. Secretary
Drama Centre
Rea Street South
Birmingham B5 6LB

Education Correspondents Group
David Fletcher
Daily Telegraph
135 Fleet Street
London EC4P 4BL

Education Welfare Officer:
Education Welfare Officer's National Association
Mr F. F. Coombes, Secretary
8 Ryeleaze
Potterne
Devizes
Wiltshire
and
Mr Colin Conway, Public Relations
87 Rockbank Road
Liverpool 13

Employment of School Leavers:
Youth Branch
Department of Employment, England and Wales
97 Tottenham Court Road
London W1P 0ER

Youth Employment Service
Board of Northern Ireland
46a Howard Street
Belfast BT1 6BH

Advisory Committee on Youth Employment for Scotland
Stuart House
Semple Street
Edinburgh EH3 8YX

Examinations:
Common Entrance Committee (for Boys)
Asley Lane
Lymington
Hampshire SO4 9YR

Common Entrance Examination
   for Girls' Schools
2 Bankfield
Kendal
Westmorland

Common Entrance
   Examinations to Public
   Schools
L. H. A. Hankey, MA,
   Secretary
138 Church Street
Kensington
London W8 4BN

*Examining Boards: General
   Certificate of Education (GCE)*
Associated Examining Board
Wellington House
Aldershot
Hampshire GU11 1BQ

Joint Matriculation Board
(covering the universities of
   Manchester, Leeds,
   Liverpool, Sheffield and
   Birmingham)
Manchester M15 6EU

Oxford and Cambridge Schools
   Examination Board
10 Trumpington Street
Cambridge
   and
Elsfield Way
Oxford

Oxford Local Examinations
Delegacy of Local Examinations
Ewert Place

Summertown
Oxford OX2 7BZ

Southern Universities Joint
   Board for School
   Examinations
(covering the universities of
   Bath, Bristol, Exeter, Reading,
   Southampton and Surrey)
Cotham Road
Bristol BS6 6DD

University of Cambridge Local
   Examinations Syndicate
Syndicate Buildings
17 Harvey Road
Cambridge CB1 2EU

University of London
   Entrance and Schools
   Examination Council
66–72 Gower Street
London WC1E 6EE

Welsh Joint Education
   Committee
245 Western Avenue
Cardiff CF5 2YX

*Examining Boards: Certificate of
   Secondary Education (CSE)*
Associated Lancashire Schools
   Examining Board
(covering Bolton, Manchester,
   Oldham, Rochdale, Salford,
   North West Derbyshire)
77 Whitworth Street
Manchester M1 6HA

East Anglian Examinations
   Board

Northern Sub-Region
(covering Bedfordshire,
    Cambridgeshire, Norfolk,
    Suffolk)
The Lindens
Lexden Road
Colchester
Essex CO3 3RL

East Midland Regional
    Examinations Board
(covering Derbyshire,
    Leicestershire, Lincolnshire,
    Northamptonshire,
    Nottinghamshire,
    Humberside)
Robins Wood House
Robins Wood Road
Aspley
Nottingham NG8 3NH

Metropolitan Regional
    Examinations Board
(covering Inner London
    Education Authority,
    Croydon, Newham)
Lyon House
104 Wandsworth High Street
London SW18 4LF

Middlesex Regional Examining
    Board
(covering Barnet, Brent,
    Ealing, Enfield, Haringey,
    Harrow, Hillingdon, Houn-
    slow, Richmond upon
    Thames)
53–63 Wembley Hill Road,
Wembley
Middlesex HA9 8BH

North Regional Examinations
    Board
(covering parts of Cleveland,
    parts of Cumbria, Durham,
    Northumberland and the
    Tyne and Wear
    Metropolitan Districts of
    Gateshead, Newcastle upon
    Tyne, North Tyneside,
    South Tyneside,
    Sunderland)
Wheatfield Road
Westerhope
Newcastle upon Tyne NE5 5JZ

North West Regional
    Examinations Board
(covering Cheshire, Lancashire,
    Isle of Man, parts of
    Cumbria, Metropolitan
    Districts of Knowsley,
    Liverpool, St Helens, Sefton,
    Wirral, Bury, Stockport,
    Tameside, Trafford, Wigan)
Orbit House
Albert Street
Eccles
Manchester M30 0WL

The South-East Regional
    Examinations Board
(covering Kent, Surrey, East
    Sussex, Bexley, Bromley,
    Kingston upon Thames,
    Merton, Richmond upon
    Thames, Sutton)
Beloe House
2 and 4 Mount Ephraim Road
Royal Tunbridge Wells
Kent TN1 1EU

Southern Regional Examinations
    Board
(covering Berkshire,
    Buckinghamshire, Dorset,
    Hampshire, Isle of Wight,
    Oxfordshire, West Sussex,
    Guernsey, Jersey, schools
    overseas of the Service
    Children's Education
    Authority)
53 London Road
Southampton SO9 4YL

Southern Sub-Region
(covering Essex, Hertfordshire,
    Greater London Boroughs
    of Barking, part of Barnet,
    Havering, Redbridge,
    Waltham Forest)
The Lindens
Lexden Road
Colchester
Essex CO3 3RL

South Western Examinations
    Board
(covering Avon, Cornwall,
    Devon, Gloucestershire,
    Somerset, Wiltshire)
23–9 Marsh Street
Bristol BS1 4BP

Welsh Joint Education
    Committee
245 Western Avenue
Cardiff CF5 2YX

West Midlands Examinations
    Board
(covering Metropolitan Districts
of Birmingham, Coventry,
    Dudley, Sandwell, Solihull,
    Walsall, Wolverhampton
    and non-Metropolitan
    Counties of Hereford and
    Worcester, Salop, Stafford-
    shire, Warwickshire)
Norfolk House
Smallbrook
Queensway
Birmingham B5 4NJ

The West Yorkshire and
    Lindsey Regional Examining
    Board
(covering Metropolitan Districts
    of Barnsley, Doncaster,
    Rotherham and Sheffield,
    parts of the Counties of
    Humberside, Lincolnshire
    and North Yorkshire and
    parts of the Metropolitan
    Districts of Bradford,
    Calderdale, Kirklees, Leeds
    and Wakefield)
Scarsdale House
136 Derbyshire Lane
Sheffield S8 8SE

Yorkshire Regional Examina-
    tions Board
(covering the former local
    authority areas of East
    Riding, Bradford, Dewsbury,
    Halifax, Huddersfield, Hull,
    Leeds, Wakefield, York)
31–3 Springfield Avenue
Harrogate
North Yorkshire HG1 2HW

Examining Boards: Technical Education

City and Guilds of London Institute
76 Portland Place
London W1N 4AA

College of Preceptors
Bloomsbury House
130 High Holburn
London WC1V 6PS

Drama Board
De Montford House
De Montford Street
Leicester LE1 7GH

Joint Committee for Higher National Certificates and Diplomas in Mathematics, Statistics and Computing and Computer Studies
Maitland House
Warrior Square
Southend-on-Sea
Essex SS1 2JY

Northern Counties Technical Examinations Council
5 Grosvenor Villas
Grosvenor Road
Newcastle upon Tyne NE2 2RU

East Midland Educational Union
Robins Wood House
Robins Wood Road
Aspley
Nottingham NG8 3NH

Royal Society of Arts

Examination Board
18 Adam Street
Adelphi
London WC2N 6AJ

Union of Educational Institutions
Norfolk House
Smallbrook
Queensway
Birmingham B5 4NB

Yorkshire and Humberside Council for Further Education
Bowling Green Terrace
Leeds LS11 9SX

Examining Boards: Scotland

Scottish Business Education Council
22 Great King Street
Edinburgh EH3 6QH

The Scottish Certificate of Education Examination Board
(for the Scottish Certificate of Education and the Scottish Certificate of Sixth Year Studies)
The Director
Ironmills Road
Dalkeith
Midlothian EH22 1BR

Scottish Technical Education Council
38 Queen Street
Glasgow G1 3DY

Examining Boards: Northern Ireland
Northern Ireland Schools Examinations Council
Examinations Office
Beechill House
Beechill Road
Belfast BT8 4RS

External Degrees:
The External Register
University of London
Senate House
Malet Street
London WC2 7H

FEVER (Friends of the Education Voucher Experiment in Representative Regions)
Mrs Marjorie Seldon, Hon. Chairman
The Thatched Cottage
Godden Green
Sevenoaks
Kent

Froebel, Friedrich:
National Froebel Foundation
2 Manchester Square
London W1

Gifted Child:
National Association for Gifted Children
Mr Henry Hollis, Director;
Mrs Margaret Branch,

Gen. Secretary
27 John Adam Street
London WC2N 6HX

Girls' Public Day School Trust (GPDST)
26 Queen Anne's Gate
London SW1H 9AN

Handicapped Children:
Action Research for the Crippled Child
Vincent House
1a Springfield Road
Horsham
Sussex

Council for Children's Welfare
183–9 Finchley Road
London NW3

Invalid Children's Aid Association
126 Buckingham Palace Road
London SW1W 9SB

National Society for Mentally Handicapped Children
Pembridge Hall
Pembridge Square
London W2 4EP

Headmasters' Conference (HMC)
Mr E. J. Dorrell, Secretary
29 Gordon Square
London WC1H 0PS

Immigrant Pupils:
The National Book League
7 Albemarle Street
London W1X 4BB

Incorporated Association of
    Preparatory Schools (IAPS)
138 Church Street
Kensington
London W8 4BN

Independent Schools
    Information Service (ISIS)
Mr Tim Devlin, Director
47 Victoria Street
London SW1H 0EQ

Initial Teaching Alphabet (i.t.a.):
Initial Teaching Alphabet
    Foundation
Alma House (Information
    Dept.)
2a Alma Road
Reigate
Surrey RH2
    for publications
Initial Teaching Publishing
    Co. Ltd.
9 Southampton Place
London WC1A 2EA

Inner London Education
    Authority (ILEA)
Mr Peter Newsam
Education Offices
County Hall
London SE1 7PB

International Baccalauréat
    Office
1 rue Albert-Gos
1206 Geneva
Switzerland

International Bureau of
    Education (IBE)
M. Leo Fernig, Director
Palais Wilson
1211 Geneva 14
Switzerland

Jewish Lecture Committee
Woburn House
Upper Woburn Place
London WC1H 0EP

Local Associations:
Education Committees Year
    Book
5 Bentinck Street
London W1M 5RN

Mature State Scholarships
Awards Branch
Department of Education and
    Science
Elizabeth House
York Road
London SE1 7PH

*Mentally Handicapped
    Children:*
National Society for Mentally

Handicapped Children
Mr G. W. Lee, OBE,
   Secretary
NSMHC Centre
Pembridge Hall
17 Pembridge Square
London W2 4EP

Multi-racial Education:
Community Relations
   Commission (CRC)
15–16 Bedford Street
London WC2E 9HX

National Association for
   Multi-racial Education
Mr Otto Polling,
The Northbrook Centre
Penn Road
Slough
Berkshire

Music Education:
Music Advisers' National
   Association
Peter Isherwood, Secretary
Coventry School of Music
Percy Street
Coventry CV1 3BY

Musical Education up to
   Thirteen
55 Farm Close
Seaford
Sussex

Music Masters' Association
J. H. Alden, Hon. Secretary
Cray Cottage

Bradfield
Reading
Berkshire

National Association of Head
   Teachers (NAHT)
Mr Robert J. Cook,
   Gen. Secretary
Maxwelton House
41 Boltro Road
Haywards Heath
Sussex

National Association of
   Inspectors and Educational
   Advisers
J. Duggon, Hon. Gen. Secretary
17 Rochester Road
Earlsdon
Coventry CV5 6AB

National Association of
   Schoolmasters/Union of
   Women Teachers (NAS/
   UWT)
Mr Terry A. Casey,
   Gen. Secretary
PO Box 65
Swan Court
Hemel Hempstead
Hertfordshire HP1 1DT

National Extension College
131 Hills Road
Cambridge CB2 1PD

National Foundation for
  Educational Research (NFER)
The Mere
Upton Park
Slough
Buckinghamshire

National Institute for Adult
  Education (NIAE)
Mr A. K. Stock, Secretary
35 Queen Anne Street
London W1M oBL

National Listening Library
49 Cumberland Place
London W1H 7LH

National Nursery Examination
  Board
Mr D. S. Wilson, Secretary
13 Grosvenor Place
London SW1X 7EN

National Union of School
  Students (NUSS)
c/o NUS
302 Pentonville Road
London N1 9LD

NUT (National Union of
  Teachers)
Mr Henry Clother (Head of
  Publicity and PR)
Hamilton House
Mabledon Place
London WC1H 9BD

The Open University
Admissions Office
PO Box 48
Milton Keynes MK7 6AB
    headquarters
Walton Hall
Bletchley
Milton Keynes
Buckinghamshire MK7 6AA

Outward Bound Trust
Mr W. H. Field, Secretary
34 The Broadway
London SW1

Parents:
Advisory Centre for Education
  (ACE)
18 Victoria Park Square
Bethnal Green
London E2 9PF

CASE (Confederation for the
  Advancement of State
  Education)
81 Rustlings Road
Sheffield S11 7AB

Gingerbread
9 Poland Street
London W1V 3DG

Home and School Council
81 Rustlings Road
Sheffield S11 7AB

Mothers in Action
9 Poland Street
London W1V 3DG

National Council for One-
  Parent Families
225 Kentish Town Road,
London NW5 2LX

Parents' National Educational
  Union (PNEU)
Miss P. Gilmour,
  Gen. Secretary
Murray House
Vandon Street
London SW1H 0AJ

Parents-Teacher Associations,
  National Confederation of
Mr John Hale, Gen. Secretary
1 White Avenue
Northfleet
Gravesend
Kent DA11 7JB

Physical Education Association
Ling House
10 Nottingham Place
London W1M 4AX

Playgroups:
Pre-School Playgroups
  Association
Alford House
Aveline Street
London SE11 5DJ

Polytechnics:
Committee of Directors of
  Polytechnics
Mr P. L. Flowerday, Secretary

309 Regent Street
London W1R 7PE

Professional Association of
  Teachers
Mr Ian Mitchell-Lambert,
24 The Strand
Derby DE1 1BE

Public Schools Bursars'
  Association (PSBA)
69 Crescent Road
Alverstoke
Gosport
Hampshire PO12 2DN

Quaker Schools:
Society of Friends
Friends House
Euston Road
London NW1 2BJ

Schools Council
160 Great Portland Street
London W1N 6LL

School Visits:
School Journey Association
  of London
J. R. Piper, Hon. Secretary
48 Cavendish Road
Clapham
London SW12 0DH

Scotland:
Scottish Education Department

New St Andrew's House
St James Centre
Edinburgh EH1 3TD
and
London Office
Dover House
Whitehall
London SW1A 2AU

Scottish Council for Health
    Education
21 Lansdowne Crescent
Edinburgh EH12 5EJ

Consultative Committee on the
    Curriculum (Scotland)
c/o Scottish Education
    Department (see above)

Scottish Council for Research
    in Education
16 Moray Place
Edinburgh EH3 6DR

Scottish Centre for Technology
12 Rose Street
Glasgow G3

Scottish Educational Film
    Association
16–17 Woodside Terrace
Glasgow G3 7XN

Scottish Sports Council
1 St Colme Street
Edinburgh EH3 6AA

Scottish Council of Social
    Service
18–19 Claremont Crescent
Edinburgh EH7 4QD

Scottish Counties of Cities
    Association
City Chambers
Edinburgh EH1 1YJ

Scottish Schoolmasters'
    Association
41 York Place
Edinburgh EH1 3HP

Scottish Secondary Teachers'
    Association
15 Dundas Street
Edinburgh EH3 6QG

Scottish Certificate of
    Education Examining Board
The Director
Ironmills Road
Dalkeith
Midlothian EH22 1BR

Scottish Technical Education
    Council
38 Queen Street
Glasgow G3

Scottish Business Education
    Council
22 Great King Street
Edinburgh EH3 6QH

General Teaching Council for
    Scotland
5 Royal Terrace
Edinburgh EH7 5AF

Scottish Universities Council
    on Entrance
Kinburn House
St Andrews
Fife KY16 9DR

Educational Institute of
   Scotland
46 Moray Place
Edinburgh EH3

Scottish Institute of Adult
   Education
Mrs B. A. Austin, Secretary
57 Melville Street
Edinburgh EH3 7HL

Scottish Union of Students
   (SUS)
30 Lothian Street
Edinburgh EH8

Society of Teachers Opposed
   to Physical Punishment
   (STOPP)
12 Lawn Road
London NW3

Student Grants
The National Union of Students
302 Pentonville Road
London N1 9LD

Technical Colleges:
Regional Advisory Council for
   Technological Education
Tavistock House South
Tavistock Square
London WC1H

UCCA (Universities Central
   Council on Admissions)

The Secretary
PO Box 28
Cheltenham
Gloucestershire GL50 1NY

UNESCO (United Nations
   Educational, Scientific and
   Cultural Organization)
7 Place de Fontenoy
75700 Paris
France
   in Britain
United Kingdom National
   Commission for UNESCO
Eland House
Stag Place
Victoria
London SW1

United Nations University
Toho Seimei Building
   (29th Floor)
15–1 Shibuye 2-chome
Shibuya-ku
Tokyo 150
Japan

*University Entrance
   Requirements:*
Association of Commonwealth
   Universities
36 Gordon Square
London WC1H 0PF

University Grants Committee
14 Park Crescent
London W1N 4DH

*Vice-Chancellors and
    Principals*
Committee of Vice-
    Chancellors and Principals
29 Tavistock Square
London WC1H 9EZ

Wales:
Schools Council Committee
    for Wales
129 Cathedral Road
Cardiff CF1 9SX

Education Committees Year
    Book
5 Bentinck Street
London W1M 5RN

Welsh Education Office
31 Cathedral Road
Cardiff CF1 9UJ

Welsh Joint Education
    Committee
245 Western Avenue
Cardiff C55 2YZ

Workers' Educational
    Association (WEA)
Mr R. J. Jeffries,
    Gen. Secretary
Temple House
9 Upper Berkeley Street
London W1H 8BY